Simple Space and Flight Experiments with Everyday Materials

Louis V. Loeschnig

Illustrated by Frances Zweifel

Sterling Publishing Co., Inc. New York

Dedication

To my beloved wife, Joanne Marie, whose love and devotion encouraged and sustained the kid in me, and to my father, Louis A. Loeschnig, whose many years in aerospace inspired me.

Edited by Claire Bazinet

Library of Congress Cataloging-in-Publication Data Available

10 9 8 7 6 5 4 3 2 1

First paperback edition published in 1999 by
Sterling Publishing Company, Inc.
387 Park Avenue South, New York, N.Y. 10016

Distributed in Canada by Sterling Publishing
℅ Canadian Manda Group, One Atlantic Avenue, Suite 105
Toronto, Ontario, Canada M6K 3E7
Distributed in Great Britain and Europe by Chris Lloyd
463 Ashley Road, Parkstone Poole, Dorset BH14 0AX, England
Distributed in Australia by Capricorn Link (Australia) Pty Ltd.
P.O. Box 6651, Baulkham Hills, Business Centre, NSW 2153, Australia
Manufactured in the United States of America

Sterling ISBN 0-8069-4246-0 Trade
0-8069-3932-X Paper

Contents

Before You Begin

The history of flight is filled with dreamers and failed attempts to fly. Born in 1452, Leonardo da Vinci, one of the earliest artists and engineers, drew flying machines and dreamed of being able to soar through the air, but that was over 400 years before manned flight became a reality.

Wilbur and Orville Wright's earliest attempts to fly, by launching kite-like gliders, were failures, but they didn't give up. At Kitty Hawk, in North Carolina, on December 17, 1903, in a craft called *Flyer,* the Wright brothers finally succeeded.

Louis Blériot (1909) became the first aviator to fly over the English Channel, from the French city of Calais to a spot near Dover, England. Sometime later, Charles Lindbergh (1927), in *The Spirit of St. Louis* (1927), and Amelia Earhart (1932) flew nonstop and solo across the Atlantic Ocean. Others soon followed.

Like flying, space travel came from man's imagination. The French writer Jules Verne (1828–1905) set down his dream of going to other worlds in a book entitled *From the Earth to the Moon*. It was a story about traveling in rockets.

Sir Isaac Newton's Law of Motion gave modern space scientists the principle that every rocket is based upon: for every action, there is an equal and opposite reaction. In 1926, an American, Robert

Goddard, built and launched the first successful fueled rocket.

In the 1940s, while the Germans developed working long-range ground missiles, the Russians worked on building larger rockets, powerful enough to thrust them towards their dream of outer space. In 1957, the Russians launched Sputnik I, the first unmanned satellite to go into orbit around the Earth. In 1961, they continued their lead in space exploration by placing the first human being in orbit, a cosmonaut named Yuri Gagarin.

Americans finally pulled ahead in the space race when, on July 20, 1969, Neil Armstrong became the first human to set foot on the moon. Later, through 1972, there were several other manned moon landings (Apollo missions). Over the years since, the U.S. has taken part in many space missions, launched many satellites and space probes, and has placed several space stations in orbit. But it is the Russians who are credited with launching and maintaining in orbit the most impressive and largest space station to date, the *Mir*.

It is the purpose of this book to give future astronauts and flight and space scientists food for thought. Here is a chance to experiment, question, think, and dream.

In this book, you'll learn about Bernoulli's Principle—without it, you'd never know the basic laws of flight. You'll design an airfoil, or airplane wing, construct a simple helicopter-like toy, learn about gravity and centrifugal/centripetal force.

In addition, you'll construct flight instruments, learn about hot-air balloons, and make a variety of gliders and planes to discover how they really work.

You'll also make your own kites—with flight and aerodynamics in mind. You'll even learn about the orbits and sizes of the planets, and do some great experiments to explain it all!

As space scientists, you'll learn about conditions on the moon, how conditions in outer space and lack of gravity affect space flight, and how astronauts reenter Earth's atmosphere and maintain orbit.

You'll design, construct, and launch a simple rocket space shuttle—and, if that's not enough, you'll learn how NASA's future astronauts are selected and trained.

Besides doing flight and space experiments, you'll learn many scientific principles of flight (aerodynamics) and space, as well as engineering, math, art and design—this book has it all!

Most of the materials you'll need in order to do the many projects in this book are inexpensive and easy to find—usually simple, everyday household items. We'll let you know, though, about the few things you may need to hunt up.

In preparation, there are a few standard supplies used often in projects and throughout this book, so why not stock up? They are: balloons (both round and oblong), paper clips (small and large), standard-size sheets of plain paper (8½ by 11 inches or A4), posterboard or light cardboard, tape, scissors, pencils, and string. General measurements given (inches to centimeters) may be approximate—not exact.

Other materials used less frequently but still important are: straws (both straight and bendable), rulers, measuring stick (yard/meter), erasers, toilet paper/paper towel tubing, various-shape boxes, jars, glue stick, freezer bags, clay, marbles, thread, aluminum foil, thermometers, rubber bands, and thumbtacks.

A few specialty items, such as small-diameter hardwood dowels and plaster of paris, may be needed, but they're not costly, and are easily available.

Finally, and most important, the experiments here were designed with care and safety in mind. When precautions need be taken for specific projects, our "Be Smart, Be Safe" bee will alert you to them.

So...what are you waiting for? Get ready, climb into the cockpit, check your instrument panel—and get ready for high-flyin' adventure!

YOU'RE ON THE AIR

Yes! You're definitely on the air in this chapter. You'll learn about the principles of flight, or Bernoulli's Law. Once you understand this, you'll know what keeps aircraft in the air.

Besides constructing many types of airfoils, or models of an airplane wing, you'll learn about air currents and how they circulate around and act on a plane's surface. This circulation of air, both fast and slow, lifts the airplane up into the upper atmosphere.

In addition, you'll construct toy helicopters, rotary motors, flying propellors, and real cardboard plane models that fly.

We've listed the simple everyday materials needed and explained everything clearly, but if you have any trouble measuring and cutting out parts, get help.

With a few simple materials, and a little effort, you'll be on the air in no time.

Ruler's Uprising

This is one ruler that will be uplifted, even do a back flip! And it's all due to Bernoulli's principle.

You need:

a strip of light cardboard, about ruler-width and half its length
tape
ruler
pencil
scissors
table

What to do:

Place the cardboard strip on the ruler so that it is touching one end and extends towards the middle. Push the strip upward a bit to form a slight arch, or curve, about an inch (1.5cm) in height. Tape both ends of the strip to the ruler.

Place the ruler on a table and balance it on the pencil. The ruler should extend about three inches (8cm) off the edge of the table.

Now, blow a steady stream of air over the top of the cardboard strip and down the length of the ruler. If nothing happens, or if the ruler just moves down the table on the pencil, adjust the balance point of the ruler on the pencil and try again.

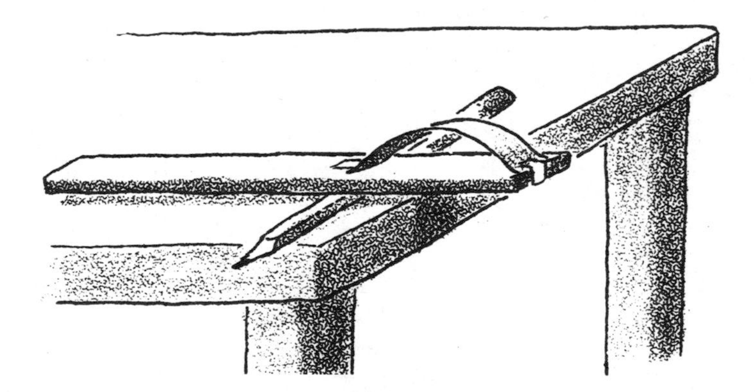

What happens:
The ruler rises, springs up, and does a back flip.

Why:
Bernoulli's principle is used when a plane lifts into the air. The same principle applies to our cardboard wing, or airfoil, taped to the ruler.

The air traveling over an airplane or cardboard wing has to travel farther and faster, so the pressure over the wing is less. Because the flow of air is slower on the wing's flat underside, it produces greater pressure and forces, or pushes, the aircraft upward.

Blowhard

Blow hard and recreate Bernoulli's Principle of Liquid Pressure. Simulate, or copy, an airplane's wing in this simple but uplifting experiment.

You need:
a strip of paper

What to do:
Place one end of the paper just below your lower lip and blow hard over the top of it.

What happens:
The paper rises and flaps in the air.

Why:
Again, a fast-moving flow of air passes over the top of the paper, producing lower pressure, while the slower airflow beneath the paper causes greater pressure. The difference is the cause of the lift, pushing the strip of paper upward.

Let's Wing It!

Do you love experiments? This one's a breeze! Design an airplane wing, or airfoil, and see how it reacts to a rapid air stream.

You need:

notebook paper
tape
large paper clip
adult help, to straighten clip

What to do:

Two pieces of notebook paper, about 4 by 5 inches or 11 by 14cm. (You can also cut a sheet of typing paper into quarters, use two now, and keep the other two quarters for the next experiment.) Keep one piece of note paper flat and form a slight arch, loop, or hill on top with the other, as shown.

Tape the curved piece of paper to the outer edges of the flat piece, and you have made a copy of an airplane wing, or airfoil.

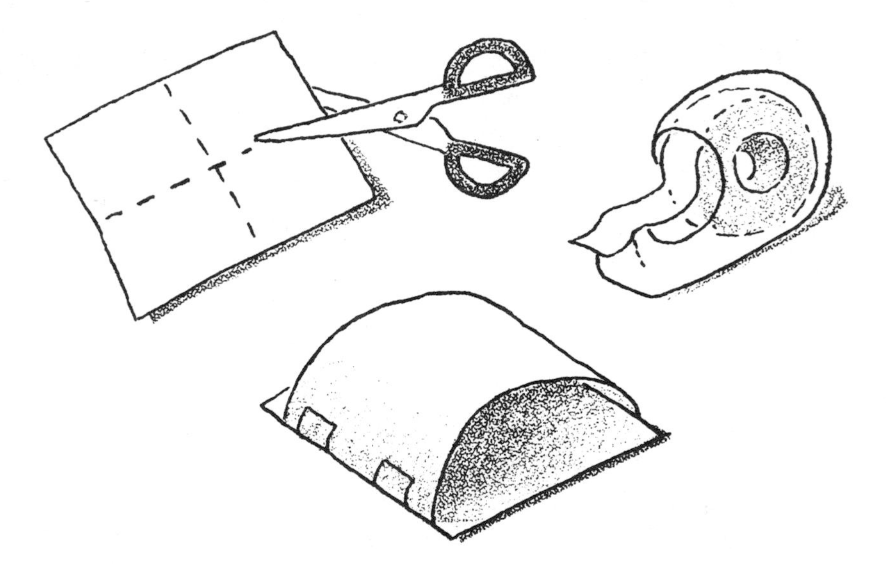

Now, carefully straighten a large paper clip (adult help may be needed) and poke it through the middle of both pieces of paper. Bend the clip slightly underneath, if needed, to hold the paper.

Gently but rapidly, blow some air *over* the short, front side of the airfoil, followed by blowing again just *underneath* it. Be careful to blow only for short periods, and to rest in between blowing (your body needs air, too!).

What happens:

When you blew a short burst of air over the curved side of the airfoil, it lifted; however, no movement was noticed when blowing a stream of air under the wing.

Why:

Again, Bernoulli's Principle, or Rule, explains it. The lower air pressure on the top of the wing and the greater pressure on the bottom caused lift. (See "Ruler's Uprising.")

Foiled Again!

This time we're going to start rolling, and then square off, and find out what happens.

You need:

notepaper
tape
straightened paper clip from "Let's Wing It!"

What to do:

From a notebook, take a small sheet of paper and roll it into a cylinder or tube, and tape it. Take another piece of paper, fold it in half, then open and fold each end to the center crease. Shape the creased sheet to form a box. Tape that, too.

Again, have someone poke the straightened paper clip into the middle of each shape and test each separately. Make certain the hole is large enough so the airfoil slides up and down the paper clip.

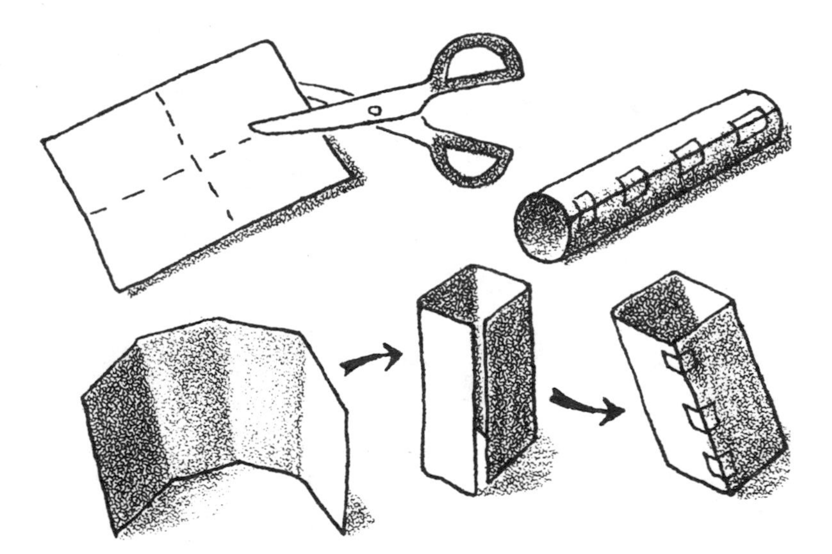

As you did in “Let’s Wing It!,” blow over the top of each shape and then under it. Again, remember to rest between blowing. Did you notice any difference in the movements between the airplane foil, the cylinder, or the box? Do you think how an airplane wing is designed is important?

What happens:
The cylinder airfoil rises very little, while the box wing does not move at all.

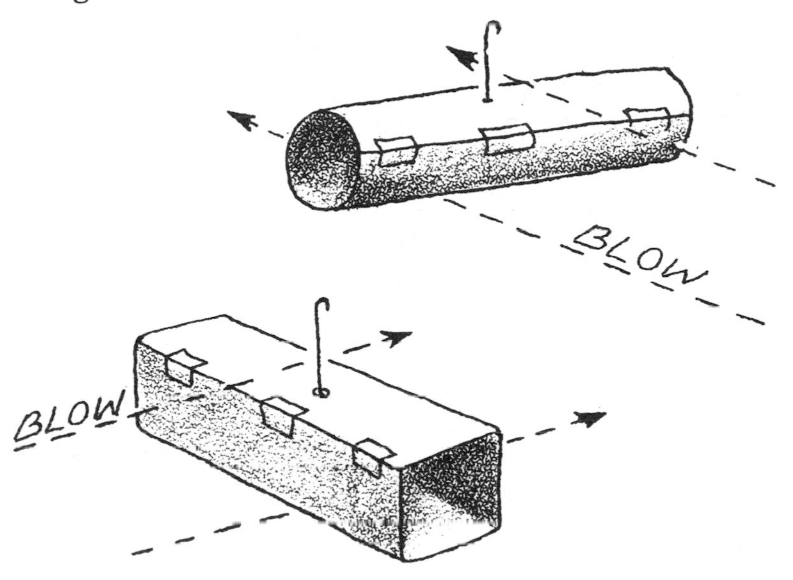

Why:
The push of air against a wing of a plane is called drag. Instead of helping the plane move smoothly through the air, it breaks up or blocks the airflow, so it holds the plane back.

This is why the design of an airplane wing is so very important. Out first airfoil created a smooth flow of air around the wing, while the curves and angles of the cylinder and box caused much drag, or breaking up and blockage of air.

Oddballs

Air affects aircraft in many ways, both lifting and pushing. See how two balloons react to each other in this oddball experiment.

You need:
2 balloons
a yard/meter length of string

What to do:
Blow each balloon up to large orange size and knot them closed. Tie a balloon to each end of the string. Hold the string up in front of your face, or arrange the string over a high fixture or lamp, so that the two balloons hang evenly, next to each other, about two inches (5cm) apart.

Now, blow a rapid stream of air between the two balloons and try to separate them more. Be sure to stop blowing and rest a few minutes between tries. You want to do your best... and not run out of breath!

What happens:
The fast-moving air stream does not separate the balloons, as you might think, but instead brings the balloons closer together.

Why:
When you blew between the balloons, the fast moving air between them caused a reduction in air pressure there, and the greater pressure on the outside of each balloon pushed them together.

Now try "High Rollers" and other experiments here for more air pressure information.

High Rollers: A Big Wind!

Sound like a Las Vegas game? No, we guarantee you won't have to gamble on this simple and successful experiment. It's just Bernoulli's Principle of Air Pressure again, demonstrating lift.

You need:

2 toilet-paper tubes
straw
a flat, steady table

What to do:

Place the two cardboard tubes about an inch (2.5cm) away from each other. With the straw, blow a steady stream of air between them. (Place the tubes on a thick, heavy book to raise the experiment higher off the table, and easier to do.)

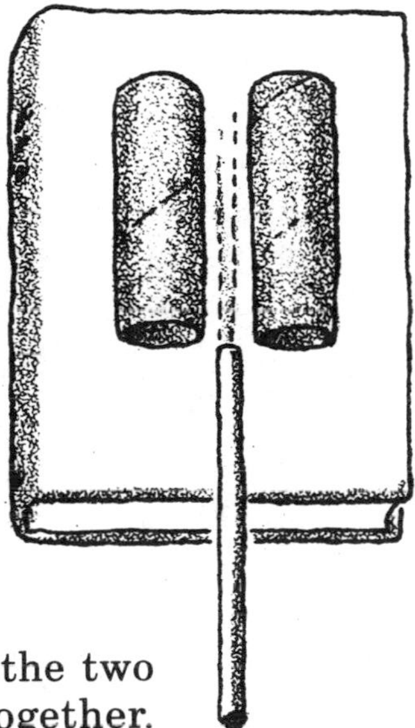

What happens:

The stream of air blown through the straw causes the two cardboard rolls to come together. (Now you know why this experiment is called "High Rollers.")

Why:

As the fast-moving air from the straw passes between the two tubes, the air pressure there is less than on the outer sides of the tubes. The difference in air pressure is enough to bring the two tubes together.

Whirlybird

In the next two experiments, you'll become an expert on helicopter flight. With a simple pencil and piece of light cardboard, you'll duplicate the effect of the spinning blades, or rotor, of a helicopter.

You need:

scissors
a pencil with an eraser
thumbtack
a strip of light cardboard, about 1¼ × 16 inches (3×40cm)

What to do:

Place the middle of the cardboard strip on the top of the pencil eraser and press the tack through the strip to attach it. Make certain the tack is in tightly, as you bend the two ends of the strip upward from the middle. Your rotor, blade, or cardboard strip should have a slight V-shape at the eraser.

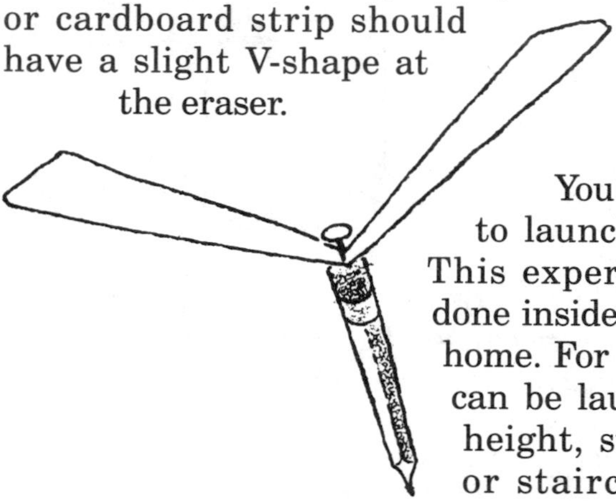

You are now ready to launch your model. This experiment can be done inside or outside the home. For best results, it can be launched from a height, such as a deck or staircase. Because high places can be dangerous, ask an adult to help—you'll want someone to witness your big launch anyway!

To do the launch properly, rapidly roll the pencil between your hands and release it. Be certain you roll and drop it the same way each time you conduct the experiment. (It should spin and turn as it drops downward.)

Do this many times, conducting many trials, before you decide how your model helicopter performs, or flies.

What happens:

With practice, your model helicopter with the cardboard strip rotor should turn and spin and whirl through the air as it gently floats downward.

Why:

Like an airplane, the rotors, or wings, of a helicopter are an airfoil and are designed to catch the slower-moving air under them rather than the fast-moving air over them.

These crowded or dense air molecules cause the rotors and the craft to be pushed upward.

The small side rotor on the tail end of the helicopter stops what is known as torque, balancing and keeping the whole craft from turning, while the main rotor helps the craft to lift and turn, according to its position.

Although our cardboard/pencil model with its rapid hand-spin thrust does not lift the model very much, it still reduces the fall rate as it descends.

Twirly-Whirlies

Twirly-what? Whirlies! In "Whirlybird," we made a simple pencil-and-paper helicopter-like toy. Now, let's replace that straight and simple blade with a circular pinwheel-and-cross rotor. Will the design of the different rotors make your model stay up in the air longer? Turn and fly better?

Do longer or wider rotors make a difference? Let's try different shapes, sizes, and widths of rotors to find out what works best.

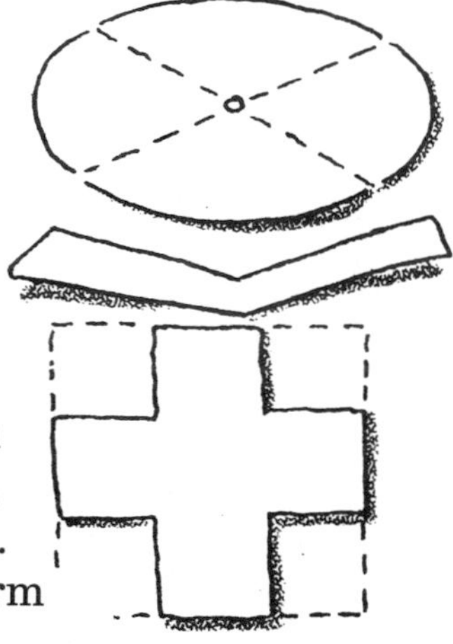

You need:

3 pencils	light cardboard
scissors	thumbtacks

What to do:

Cut a circle between 4½ and 8 inches (11–20cm) in diameter from the light cardboard. Cut four slits opposite each other in *towards* the center, but leave the center uncut. Fold one side of each slit to form a pinwheel.

Next, cut a strip 2 by 8 inches (5×20cm) long and fold the strip in the center to form a V. Last, cut a 6-inch (15cm) square of cardboard and cut out 2-inch (5cm) squares from each corner to form a cross. Turn the cross ends up.

Now, tack the middle of each cardboard rotor to the top of a pencil eraser. Make certain the thumbtack is securely in place on all three models.

To launch, rapidly roll a pencil between your hands and release it. Again, see "Whirlybird" for help and hints!

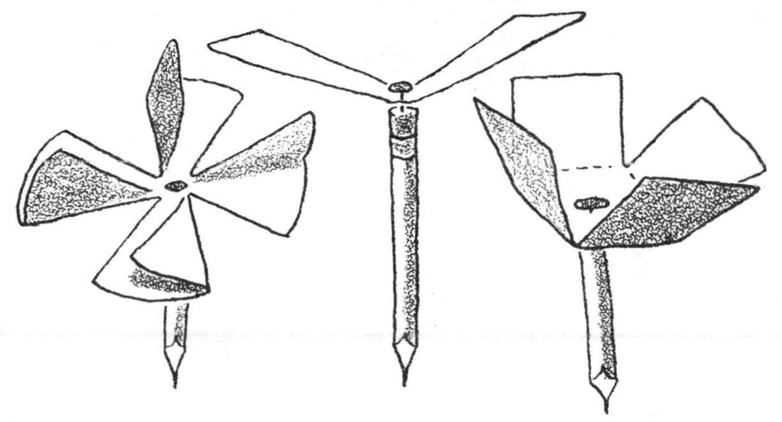

What happens:
With our test models, the 2 by 8 inch (5×20cm) strip worked fairly well but was somewhat clumsy. The pinwheel airfoil was very clumsy, did not turn or rotate, and fell to the ground without catching the air currents. However, the 6-inch (15cm) cross rotor flew very well, with smooth and gentle spinning, or rotation, as it softly fell to the ground.

Why:
The cross rotor was probably more like a real helicopter's airfoil than the other models. The wide blades with the four upturned ends, when rotated by hand, caught the denser, closer air underneath it and reduced the rate of drag from air holding it back as it fell to the ground. See "Whirlybird."

What now:
Do this same experiment, but see if you can make a perfect airfoil, or helicopter rotor, by adjusting the variables—other things that can affect spinning and flight.

For example, will longer or wider rotors make a difference? Or heavier or lighter paper or cardboard? Will making a drive shaft or spinning launcher help? In the next experiment, we'll find out!

Rotor Motor

You can make a jet-propelled, helicopter-like rotor, or blade, whirl, using nothing but 100 percent balloon power.

You need:

cardboard paper towel tube
2 large oblong balloons
one ¼-inch wooden dowel, 18 inches (45cm) long
scissors
paper clip
tape
a helper

What to do:

Ask an adult to help by using a sharp scissors tip to punch two holes completely through the tube, through both sides, at a point midway along its length. The holes need to be exactly opposite each other so that an inserted dowel will fit right across. Place the dowel through the holes in the tube and turn, or rotate, the tube on the dowel many times until it spins freely.

Next, blow up one of the oblong balloons, twist and clip it, and carefully tape it to one end of the tube. (Be sure to fasten it well.)

Blow up the second balloon, twist and clip it, and fasten it to the other end of the tube, making certain the balloon opening is facing opposite the first balloon.

Now, get ready for the action! To do two things at once, you'll need the help of your assistant.

While your helper carefully takes the paper clip off one of the balloons and holds the end of it closed, you do the same—and, at a given signal, both of you release your balloons.

What happens:
As soon as you release the balloons, the tube whirls and spins.

Why:
The rush of air from the balloons mounted on opposite ends of the tube pushes them forward, turning the tube around the dowel. The air being expelled by the balloons causes this push. Sir Isaac Newton's third law of motion explains it best: for every action there is an equal and opposite reaction. The reaction of the balloons is to move forward. What would happen if the two balloons were placed on the dowel with their neck openings in the same direction?

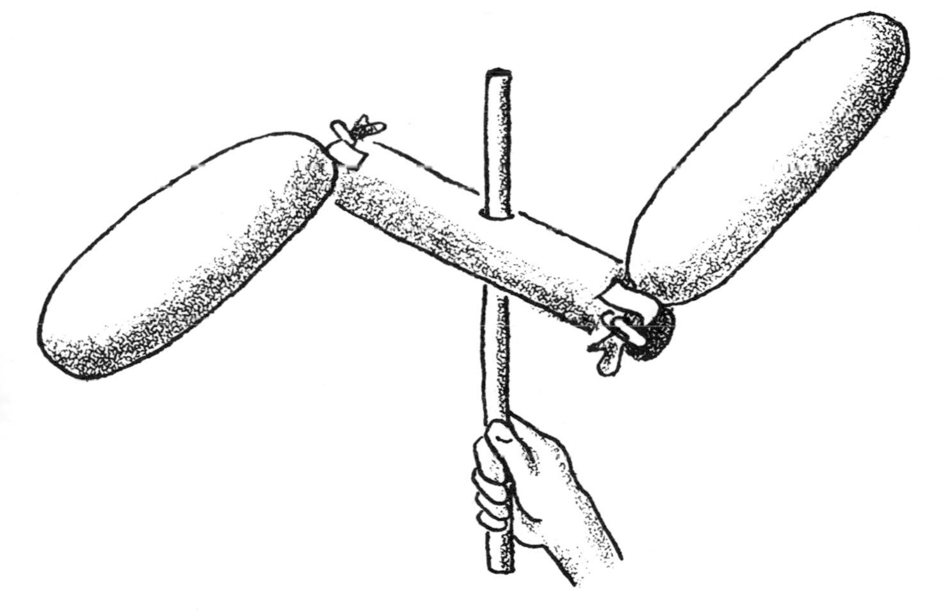

An American Yank

We felt like the Wright brothers when we first experimented with this spinning airfoil, or helicopter. We used cardboard, plastic, and other materials for the blades, or rotor, and people laughed, like they did at the Wright brothers' first "airplane," when our first efforts flopped, bounced, and plopped on the floor.

However, after long hours of work and many tryouts, we succeeded in putting together the right combination of materials. So here we have for you the best and easiest model to make. If you are careful to follow the clear and simple directions we've given here, we won't let you down. Now, it's time to pull some strings, give your helicopter a good old fashioned American yank, and watch it take off. We're confident you'll be flying high in no time!

You need:

thread, about 26 inches (70cm)
light cardboard, 2 by 3 inches (5×7cm)
construction paper, 6 inches (15cm) square
scissors
pencil with eraser
thumbtack
tape

What to do:

Wrap the cardboard rectangle around the pencil to form a cylinder and tape it. Make certain the tube is loose enough for the pencil to turn inside it (drive shaft).

Next, cut 2-inch (5cm) squares from each corner of the construction paper, forming a cross (see "Twirly-Whirlies"). Place this cross-shaped rotor on top of the pencil eraser and fasten it with the tack. Make certain the tack is in tight enough so the rotor won't fall off. Bend the blades upward for better flight.

Last, place just the pencil point, or about an inch (2.5cm) of pencil, into the drive-shaft cylinder. Wrap the thread around the pencil above it, as you would wind kite string around a stick—keeping it smooth, straight, and tight.

Although it is not necessary, it's best to test-fly this experimental craft from a higher point to a lower area to observe the results. Again, ask for help if needed.

Pull the thread rapidly but smoothly and watch your helicopter turn with a whirr and lift into the air.

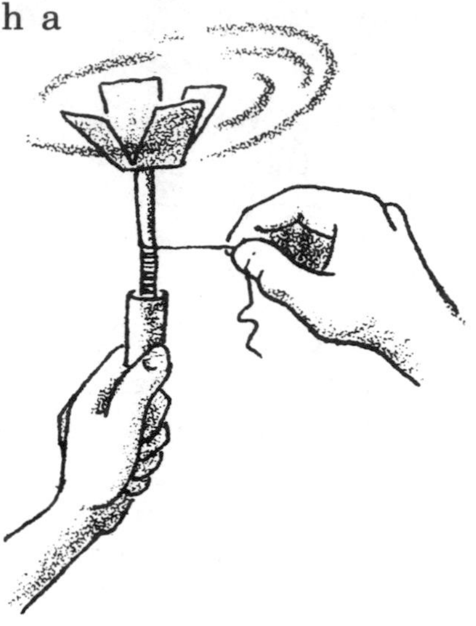

If your helicopter doesn't work as it should, look for these variables, or other things that could be affecting its upward flight:

1) Is the thread wound too high on the pencil?
2) Is the pencil too deep in the drive shaft?
3) Is the tack holding the rotor lose or crooked, or still tight and in place?
4) Is the drive shaft too tight around the pencil?
5) Did you use string instead of thread? (String fibers are rough and cause drag by catching on the drive shaft and pencil.)

What happens:

As you pull the thread away from around the pencil, the pencil is made to rotate, or turn, making a gradual but noticeable whirring sound, and the craft lifts into the air.

Why:

The rapid action of the rotating, or spinning, pencil causes the moving rotor blades to lift up in reaction to the air being forced or pushed down.

I'm Banking On You!

Would you like to make the kind of instrument that helps pilots determine an airplane's position in flight? The *artificial horizon* will tell you whether you are flying level, or banking, or tilting, right or left. You're bound to crash in on the fun.

You need:

shoe box lid
plastic sandwich or freezer bag
2 permanent markers (different colors)
scissors
short bolt with nut, or other fastener
paper hole punch (optional)
tape
ruler

What to do:

Flatten and cut the ends off the shoe box lid and cut the flat, rectangular piece of cardboard in half. Cut one of the halves an inch (3cm) shorter (1).

Cut a 3-inch (8cm) square from the plastic bag. With one of the marker pens, draw a straight line across the center of the piece (2).

Now, cut a 2¾-inch (7cm) circle from the center of the longer piece of cardboard and tape the clear plastic piece with the line on it to one side. Again, make certain the line is centered in the middle (3).

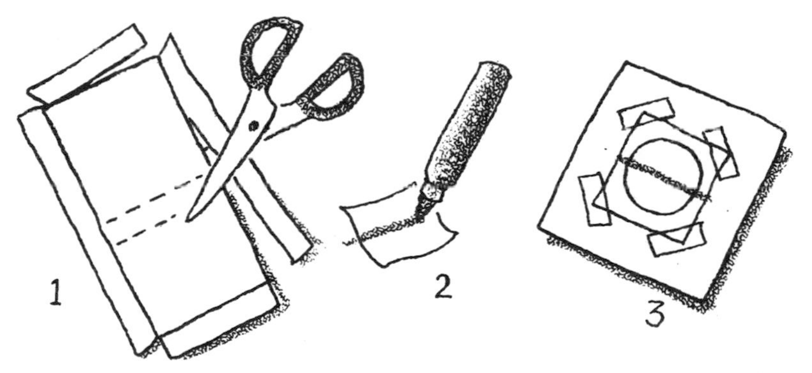

On the second, shorter piece of cardboard, draw a different-colored line. It should be in the center, so as to divide it. Now draw a 90-degree straight line vertically or straight up from the center of the other line. You should have what looks like an upside down T.

Last, place the two cardboard pieces together—the window-lined piece on top of the inside shorter T-piece. Make certain both lines are matched up with each other.

Have someone punch a hole in the top center pieces of the cardboard, as you would a hanger on a picture, and position the bolt and nut (or fastener) in it.

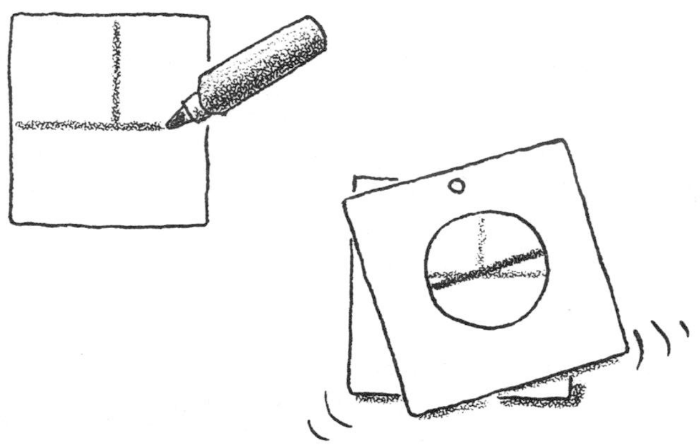

The back (shorter) piece should move freely back and forth, much like a pendulum on a clock. Your flight instrument is now ready to be tested.

The line you drew on the plastic window represents the wing, while the cardboard with lines attached to the window shows the horizon, the line between the earth and sky.

Hold the attached longer piece level with the floor and slowly but gradually tip the instrument to the right and then to the left.

What happens:
When tilting, if the horizon line is below the wing, the airplane is headed upward. If the line is above the wing line, the plane is angled downward.

Why:
A real artificial horizon helps a pilot navigate accurately even if he or she cannot see ahead. It tells the pilot whether the plane is going up, down, or flying level.

The instrument shows two lines, one of which represents the horizon, the other the wing. The horizon line is balanced by a gyroscope or a spinning wheel that keeps the horizon line level with the real horizon. This instrument is so accurate that it keeps the two horizon lines steady, even if the airplane is not.

NOTE: Your artificial horizon must be matched up, line for line, carefully in order to register correctly, to give you an accurate reading.

Meter-Made

Make an aneroid barometer, which is similar to an airplane's altimeter (altitude meter). Although your liquidless barometer won't measure altitude above sea level, it will teach you the highs and lows of air-pressure changes.

You need:

16 oz. wide-mouth jar
straw
tape
large balloon
scissors
ruler
clay

What to do:

Cut the neck off the balloon and make a one-inch (3cm) cut on its side. Open it up and stretch it over the mouth of the jar, as you would spread skin over a drum. It should be put on tight, but not *too* tight. Done correctly, it will not slip off the mouth of the jar but will form an airtight seal.

Next, place the straw in the middle of the balloon skin and carefully and gently tape it.

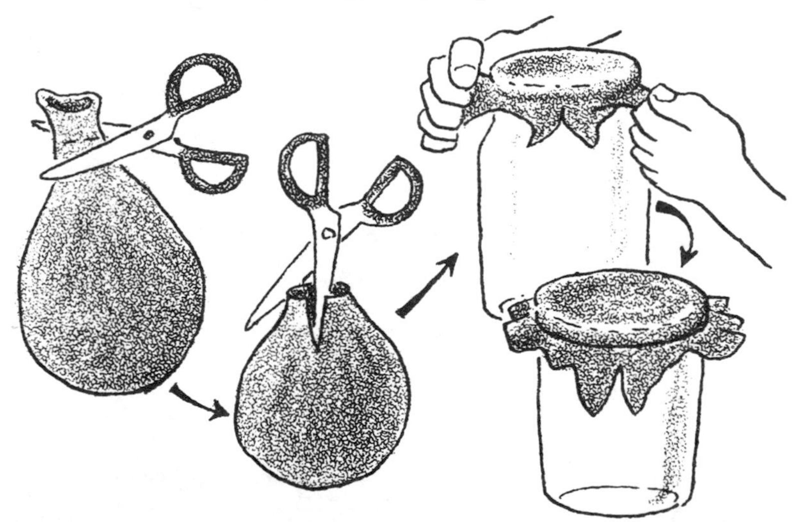

Last, form a ball with the clay and stick the end of the ruler with the lower numbers into it. The clay will form a stand for your ruler-scale. Place the ruler close to the straw and record any numbered up and down movements.

What happens:
The straw will move up or down to record any air pressure changes in the jar.

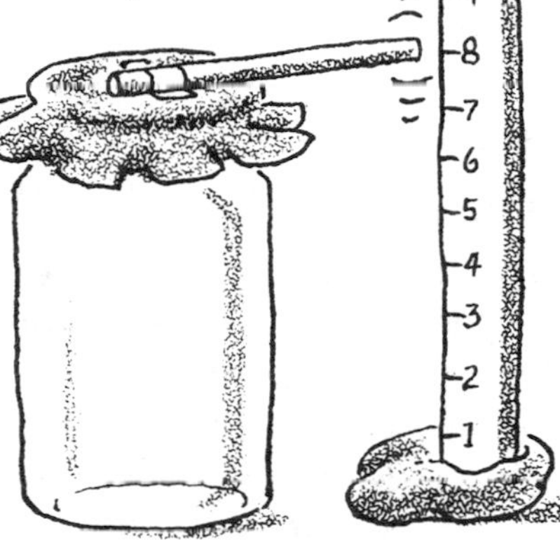

Why:
When the straw moves upward on the ruler, the pressure is higher; when it falls, the pressure is lower.

The aneroid barometer you made is similar to an airplane's altimeter, but it has no liquid in it. Too, unlike the airplane's device, it only shows altitude changes above sea level.

As a plane ascends, or climbs, the air pressure becomes less and is recorded as a drop on the altimeter. Air pressure at sea level exerts a greater force and affects all things on Earth.

NOTE: In order to show accurate barometric pressure changes, keep your barometer safe and undisturbed in a sheltered area for an extended, or long, period of time.

Tailspin

You'll go into a tailspin when you see how an airplane rudder controls left and right turns.

You need:

lightweight cardboard, 10 by 12 inches (25×30cm)
ruler
pencil
scissors
a medium to large size toothpaste carton
2 thumbtacks
2 paper clips
adult help
nail

What to do:

In the middle of the piece of cardboard, draw a line with the ruler, about 8 inches (20cm) long. Place the ruler next to the line and draw the remaining lines around it to form the outline of the ruler. You should have drawn a long rectangle.

When done, you want an airplane pattern with a wingspan on each side that measures 2 by 4 inches (5×10cm). So, about 2 inches (5cm) down from the top of the rectangle, draw a line 4 inches (10cm) long out to the side. Do this on both sides of the body. From the end of these wing lines, draw 2-inch long (5cm) lines parallel to the body of the plane, the width of the wings. Then fill in the remaining lines on both sides to complete the wing section.

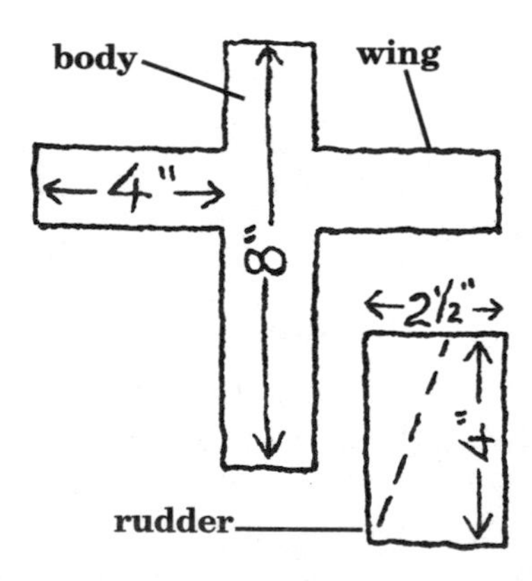

With the remaining cardboard, cut out a rectangle that measures 2½ by 4 inches (6×10cm). This piece will represent the rudder. Now cut out both plane and rudder patterns. Cut a slanted piece from one side of the rudder.

Align the plane pattern and attach it with thumbtacks to the narrow side of the toothpaste carton.

Pull out the main end flap of the toothpaste carton (near the tail-end of the airplane pattern) and attach the rudder to the flap with a paper clip (with the straight side of the rudder facing away from the airplane pattern).

Sharp tool!

Puncture wounds can be dangerous, so get an adult to open and carefully straighten part of a paper clip. The straight end of the paper clip needs to be pushed through the middle underside of the box (underneath your attached plane pattern and behind the wing) and up through the top side. (A small nail may be helpful in starting the holes.) For safety, and to keep the plane on the clip, the straight, exposed part of the paper clip should be bent downward.

Your model plane is finished and is now ready to be tested.

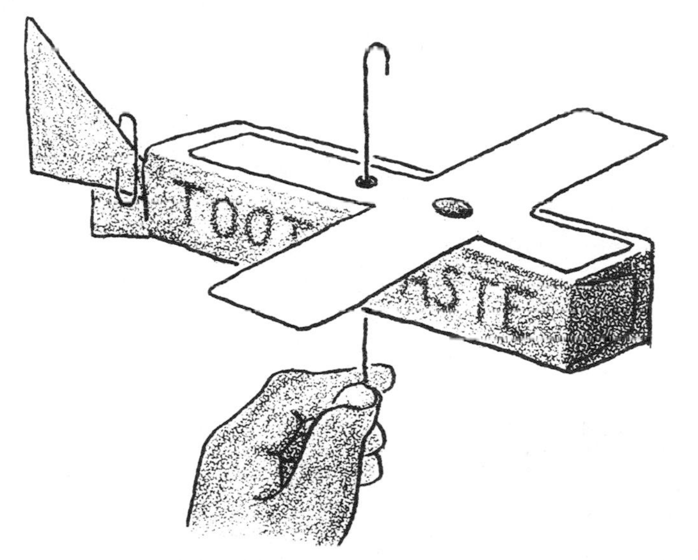

To do this, look behind the model and push the rudder towards the right wing. Now, position the plane, the front towards you, while carefully holding the underside paper clip, and gently blow a stream of air towards the rudder.

Now, repeat this action while reversing the rudder as far as it will go to the left. (Since the rudder is attached to the right side of the flap, it will be necessary for you to push and press it to the left as much and as hard as you can.

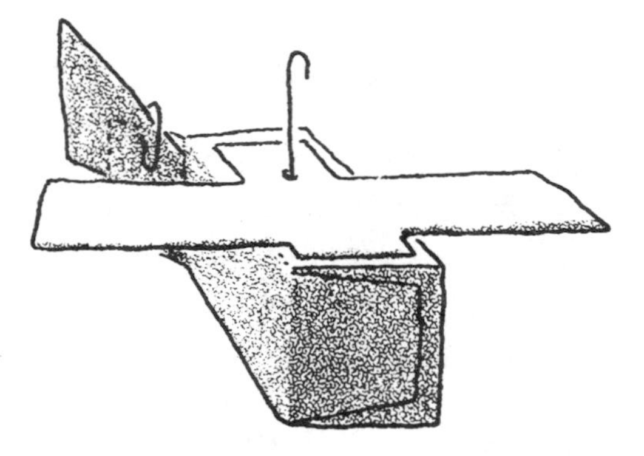

What happens:
Blowing on the rudder at different angles will move the model plane right to left.

Why:
When you blew a stream of air against the rudder while it was turned to the right, the air hit its right side, turning the plane's nose to the right. When you blew a stream of air against the rudder while it was moved to the left, the air force again pressed against it, this time moving the plane's nose to the left.

*Keep your model airplane for more flight experiments (see "Flap-Happy").

Flap-Happy

In "Tailspin," you made a model airplane with a rudder that controlled left and right turns, called "banking." Here, you'll go one step further and cut flaps in the wings of your model airplane. These flaps will further control turns. In addition, you'll learn a lot about giving right-left directions—right? No, left!

You need:

"toothpaste-carton" airplane
pencil
scissors
ruler

What to do:

Using your "Tailspin" model, mark off a 2-inch (4cm) space on each side of the wings, making certain the marked space is in the same area on both wings.

Now, draw vertical or straight lines about an inch long (2cm) from the end marks of each two-inch area on each wing. These will represent the wing flaps, or *ailerons*. Now make a cut on each vertical line—you should make two cuts on one wing; then two cuts on the other. By folding, you will now have movable flaps on each side of the wings.

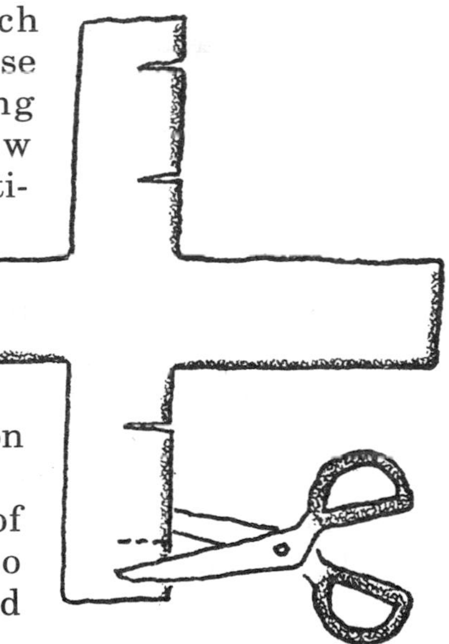

Look from the back of your model's wings to determine right wing and left wing. Turn the right aileron up and the left aileron down and the rudder to the right. Now blow a steady stream of air from the front against the upturned flap. Which way does the airplane turn? Remember, the name for right-wing/left-wing turn is based on position from the *back* of your model, not from the front. Remember, also, to line up the model with your right and left hand.

Now, turn the flaps in the opposite direction, with the left aileron up and the right aileron down and the rudder pushed to the left. Again, blow a stream of air towards the front of the model. Which way does the airplane turn?

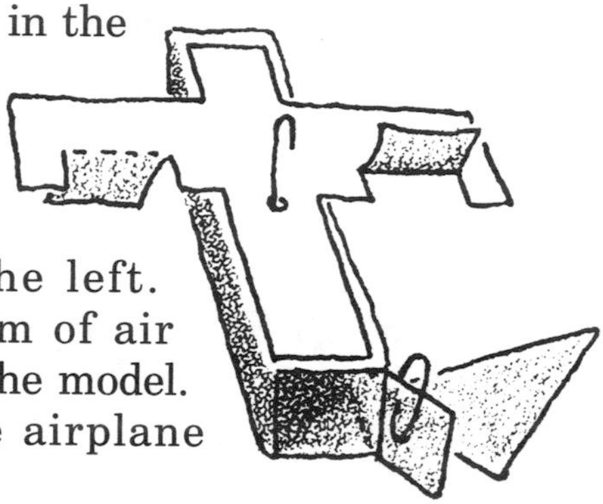

What happens:

When you turned the right aileron up and the left aileron down and the rudder to the right, the model turned to the right. The plane turned to the left when the left aileron was up and the right aileron was down and the rudder was pushed to the left.

Why:

Again, as in "Tailspin," the model turned to the right when the right aileron was up and the rudder was pushed to the right. The plane turned to the left when the left aileron was up and the rudder was pushed to the left.

Again, in both cases, the air stream hit the flat surfaces that were turned towards it and moved the model accordingly.

What's All the Flap About?

You know something about aileron and rudder flaps from testing a practically stationary or non-movable model. Now, we'll go further. You'll throw and fly a real model with movable flaps. You'll even add a stabilizer—the horizontal, flat piece of the tail—to your experimental aircraft. Both will make your model even more interesting.

You need:

light cardboard, 12 inches (30cm) square
pencil
ruler
scissors
paper clips
tape

What to do:

Draw the parts of your model plane. First, draw a 10-inch (25cm) long rectangular box (ruler width) across the middle of the cardboard. When folded as shown, this will form the fuselage, or the body of the plane, with slits for the wing and stabilizer pieces.

Add a tailpiece to the fuselage by drawing a 3-inch (8cm) line up from the top left end of the rectangle and then a 2-inch (5cm) line across to the right, towards the front of your model. Finally, draw a line diagonally downward, to meet the top of the rectangle. This up-and-down part of the tailpiece, attached to the fuselage, is the rudder of your plane.

For the wing, draw another ruler-width 10-inch (25cm) rectangular box.

Next, draw another, shorter rectangle. Make it about 2 by 5 inches (5×12.5cm). This will represent the plane's elevator, or stabilizer; it is the flat and even part of your model's tailpiece.

To assemble your model plane, cut out the fuselage (body) with its attached rudder, the wing, and the stabilizer (flat part of tail assembly).

Make a crease, or fold, down the center of the fuselage. Fasten it with a paper clip. The clip can be removed later, as the plane is further assembled.

Now, 2 inches (4cm) from the front of the plane, in the middle of the folded-over fuselage, draw a 2-inch (4cm) line. Here, have an adult cut through the doubled-over fuselage to form a slit.This is where the wing will go. Make a similar line and slit towards the back of the plane, at the base of the rudder. Insert the stabilizer and the wing into their slits and adjust them. Reinforce the positions of your stabilizer and wing by taping them to the fuselage.

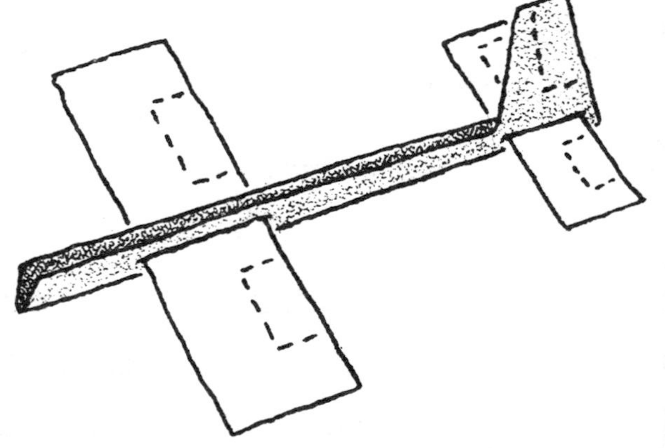

If your model's parts are large and it flies awkwardly, streamline it. Cut the areas at the ends of the wings, rudder, and stabilizer to round them off. Cut the nose at an angle, trimming it, and place 4 or 5 paper clips on the nose assembly to balance and add weight to the model while removing any unnecessary clips on the fuselage.

Last-minute trimming and the adjusting of the weights is necessary to make your model stable, steady, and most important, able to fly well.

Before cutting flaps in your plane's wing, rudder, and stabilizer, take it outside and test it for flight. How you launch, or throw, your plane and the scientific methods you use are important variables. See "Flight Pattern" for help.

Once your plane flies well, cut flaps an equal distance apart on the wings, stabilizer, and rudder. Adjust flaps up on the stabilizer to make your plane climb, or down to make it dip. Adjust ailerons (wing flaps) and rudder (flap at back) to the left or right to make turns. Let it fly!

What happens:

Your model plane flies differently depending on how the flaps are positioned.

Why:

When you turned the left wing's aileron up and rudder flap to the left, the air stream pushed towards the flaps and turned the model in that direction. The opposite applies when the right aileron and rudder are in the opposite direction.

Also, the movable flap in the stabilizer—the flat tailpiece—moves the plane according to how the air stream is hitting it. When lowered, the plane dives; when raised, it ascends, or climbs.

FLIGHT PATTERN

When you take your plane outside and throw it, you must remember that this is a scientific experiment. Like all scientific experiments, launching your model plane must be conducted scientifically. If your plane does not fly well or does not fly at all, there's probably a scientific explanation.

Again, go back to "What's All the Flap About?" Did you correctly trim and adjust the weights on your plane? Did you streamline the wings, body (fuselage), rudder, and the stabilizer by cutting rounder corners? If not, your plane may be too clumsy and awkward to fly.

Adjust paper clips on the nose of your plane and do not be afraid to add more, take away some, reposition clips, or add larger and heavier clips.

Remember, this is an experiment and you want to know which features will make your model fly best. Be adventurous and don't be afraid to try different things to make your plane fly longer, higher, and straighter.

Also, you might want to try making different-sized models with different designs by slightly changing the directions in "What's All the Flap About?" Larger planes usually glide longer distances and turn less. The possibilities for having your plane do what you want it to do are endless.

To make the best throws, find the center of gravity of your plane. If it has clips on its nose, place a finger and your thumb under the wing. When your model does not fall off your fingers and is perfectly balanced, you'll have found the center of gravity. This is where you should hold your plane; for ours, it was just behind the wing.

When you hold your plane at its balancing point, you'll get straighter, smoother, and longer flights every time.

So have fun! Your plane experiments will never bore you, but instead leave you flying high with excitement.

A Prop-er Engine: A Wheel Deal!

Modern jet planes use a mixture of fueled, hot, compressed rushing air to turn a series of wheeled fans on rods, or axles (called turbines).

This compressed, or flattened and pressed, air is then forced out of the plane's tail and it pushes, or thrusts, the craft forward. Early turboprop planes used propellers and turbines to do the same job, but not as well as modern jet crafts. Find out how early jet-prop planes worked in this simple, easy, and fun experiment—it's a wheel deal!

You need:

one medium cup with plastic lid (from fast food place, save yours!)
lump of clay (size of a large marble)
rubber band
cardboard
scissors
ruler
straw
tape

What to do:

Cut a rectangular section in the middle side of the cup that extends halfway down its sides. Poke a hole in the middle of the bottom of the cup and cut the flap off the straw hole in the plastic lid.

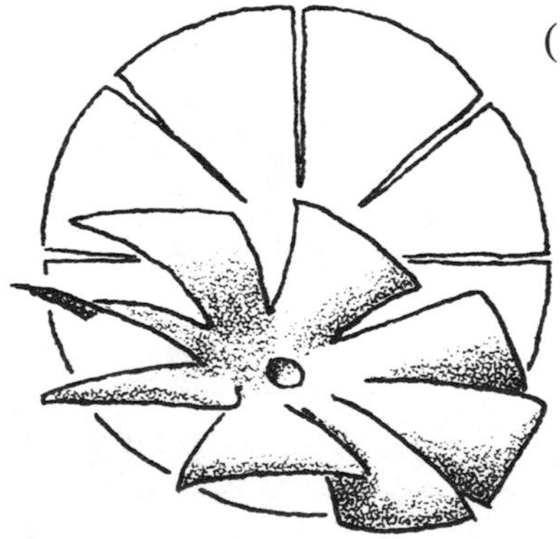

Draw two circles 3 inches (8cm) in diameter on the cardboard and divide each into eight parts, like circles used for teaching fractions.

Next, make ¾ cuts on the lines in the circles and bend the sections back and forth to represent the blades of a fan. Use tape to reinforce cuts and repair any tears.

Poke holes in the middle of the circular fans and push the straw through them. Each fan should be in the middle of the straw and about 2 inches (5cm) from the other.

Fit the fan-and-straw assembly through the bottom hole of the cup while securing the plastic lid and straw into the top. Test the assembly to see if it turns easily. If not, cut larger holes to accommodate the straw, so that it will turn freely.

To make the propeller, cut a 1×5-inch (2.5 ×13cm) propeller-shaped piece out of the cardboard.

Cut small slits into the center of each side and gently bend each part in opposite directions. This will give the propeller its third-dimension-al shape.

Assemble the propellor by wrapping the rubber band around the straw securely, where it pokes up through the lid. This will act as a buffer between the propeller and the lid, so that the propeller will

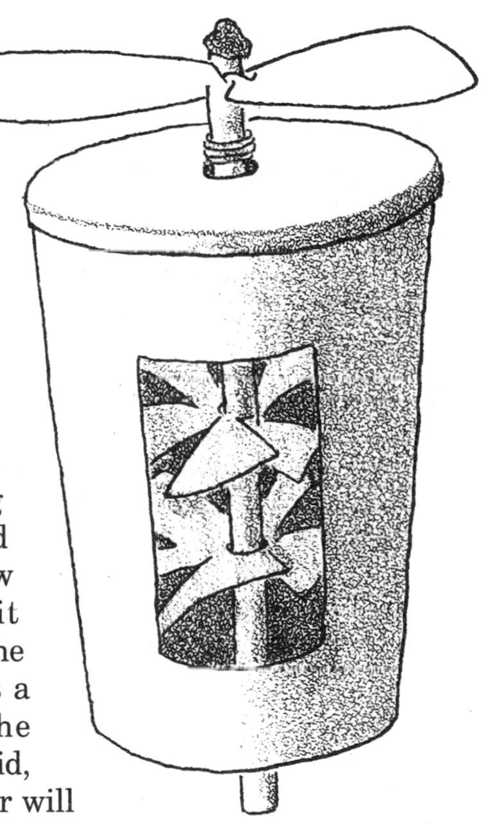

stay forward and turn more freely. Next, place the propeller on the end of the straw (it will be necessary to poke a hole in the middle of the propeller), in front of the wrapped rubber band.

Finally, secure the propeller in place by shaping a nose for your plane out of clay and pushing it into place on the straw in front of the propeller.

Now you are ready to test your model jet prop. Blow a steady stream of air to the sides of the propeller and watch what happens.

What happens:

By blowing a stream of air to the sides of the propeller, the compressor-turbine fanned parts are turned around.

Why:

Although our experimental turboprop model is fun to make and test, it does not necessarily show how a real turboprop works. Our model essentially was made to show how the movement of turbine parts is needed in the jet-propulsion process. In a real turboprop engine, the turbines turn the propellers, while in our model it is the propeller that turns the turbine parts.

Again, in a modern jet engine, incoming air at the front of the plane is compressed, or squeezed together, by engine parts. The jet's fuel is ignited or burned in a chamber and the hot gases are blown out of the rear of the plane. The thrust, or the forward push of the plane, is explained by one of Newton's three laws of motion, put forth in the year 1687, that every action has an equal and opposite reaction.

Forward, March!

In the last experiment, we learned about Newton's law of motion. Simply put, it states that for every action there must be an equal and opposite reaction.

When rushing fueled air in a jet plane's engine is activated or ignited, the heated air that is released from the rear of the plane pushes the plane forward. This is a perfect example of thrust. We can further see this law in rockets and planes by doing a few important but simple experiments:

You need:

balloons
masking tape
standard sheet of paper
scissors

What to do:

First, blow up a few balloons and release them. When you blow the balloons up and let them go, the air comes out of the neck and propels them forward. A similar reaction occurs in planes and rockets.

You can make a simple rocket (you'll construct and develop more interesting rockets later on) by rolling a piece of paper into a cylinder and taping it.

Next, cut a piece of masking tape about 6 inches (15cm) long and stick it on the neck of the balloon. Forming a bridge with the balloon and tape, stick the sides of the tape to the cylinder. You should be able to put your finger in the space between the tape and the cylinder. Also, the neck of the balloon should be facing the inside of the cylinder but with the opening out far enough to allow you to blow into it.

Now, blow a stream of air into the balloon and hold the end until it is ready to be released. If the tape starts to loosen or the balloon is stuck hard to the tape, readjust the tape or the balloon or start over. When ready, release the balloon and watch what happens.

The simple cylinder rocket is propelled forward as the air released from the neck of the balloon rushes through it.

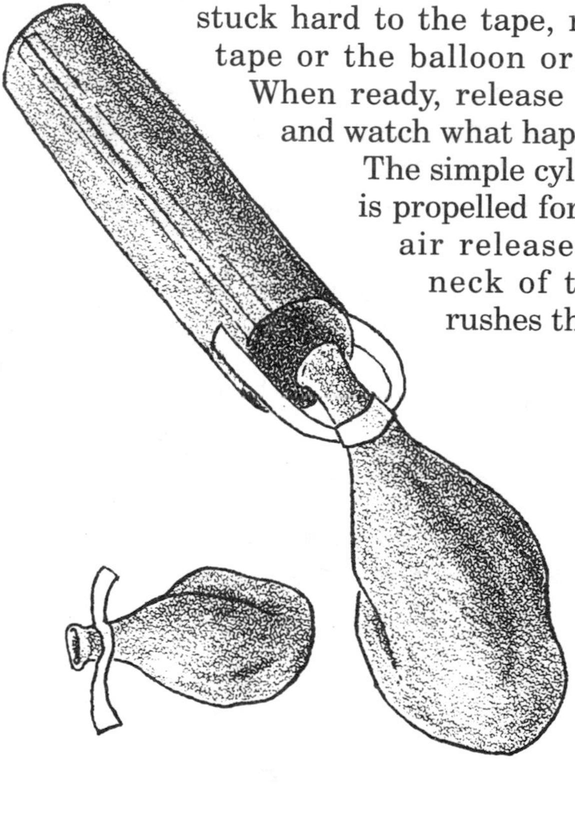

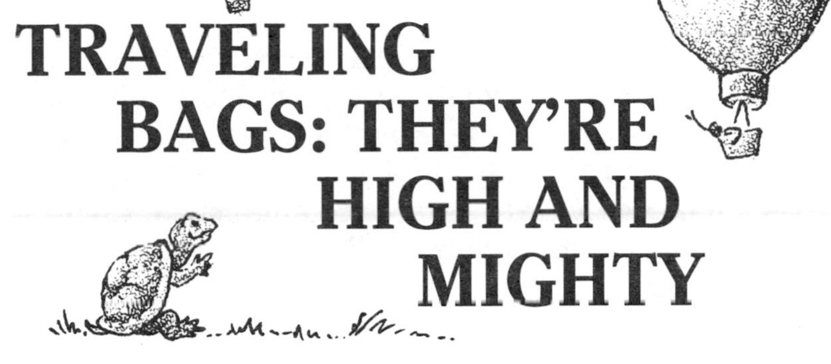

TRAVELING BAGS: THEY'RE HIGH AND MIGHTY

Mankind could never keep eyes, and feet, on the ground. Watching birds soaring high above, people dreamed of joining them—and never stopped trying.

As early as the 1600s, long before the invention of the airplane, people talked of attaching baskets to flying spheres or balls. For years, they experimented with such balloons and large bags filled with lighter-than-air gases. Finally, in 1783, a French papermaker, Etienne Montgolfier, was credited with the first successful man–balloon launch—using hot air.

Air expands when heated, becoming lighter than the air surrounding it. One problem with early hot-air balloons was that the air inside would cool off. Then came the propane burner, which could be made to hang beneath a balloon, and the problem was solved.

Today, hot-air ballooning enthusiasts still enjoy just floating quietly on air currents. But balloons have been used to explore the atmosphere, gather data and weather information, even communicate. So, get ready for some air-raising experiences with air pressure and heated and expanded air, and learn about communication using helium balloons.

Airbag Balancing Act

You'll have lots of fun learning how hot air behaves in this enjoyable, magical experiment. It's easy to put together and involves everyday materials you'll find around the house. However, you will need an assistant and a steady hand.

CAUTION: Adult assistance is recommended. Involves work with a lighted lamp bulb. Also, keep materials for next experiment.

You need:

2 paper lunch bags
2 paper clips
an assistant
a ruler
string, 12 inches (30cm)
scissors
a pencil
a table lamp

What to do:

Open fully the two lunch bags. Place a paper clip on each flat, closed end of the bags.

Cut the string in half and tie each piece securely to each paper clip on each bag. Finally, tie each stringed paper bag to each end of the ruler. You have now made a simple balance.

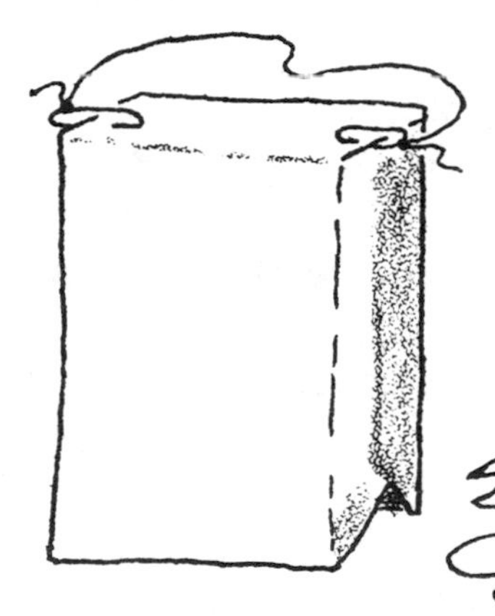

Have someone remove the shade from a table lamp. The lamp should be low enough so you or your assistant can hold one end of the bag-balance over it.

Now, you or your assistant should balance the ruler on the end of the pencil. When equally balanced, notice how both sides are the same.

For a few minutes, hold one of the bags slightly above the heated bulb. Again, you'll need a steady hand and you and your partner will need to watch what happens. Can you or your helper tilt one end of the balance, with the heated bulb, so that it will fall?

Hot bulb!

What happens:

After a few minutes, one end of your bag-balance should slightly tip or lean to one side and finally fall.

Why:

The molecules of warmed air rising from the lighted bulb are moving very fast and are expanded or farther apart. It is this warmer, expanded air that is responsible for pushing against the bag and slightly lifting it.

Toy Balloons and Old Bags Still Rise to the Occasion

Again, you can simply and easily prove that air expands when heated—very hot news for toy balloons and old bags (hot-air balloon bags, that is). So go ahead and blow up a few balloons and measure some hot air. We know you're bursting with excitement. It's definitely nothing to take lightly.

You need:

balloon
string
tape measure (or string and ruler)
lamp or other heat source
adult help
pencil and paper

What to do:

Blow up a balloon and tie it off with a string. Measure the circumference of the balloon (distance around the widest part). Write down the measurement. Now, with the help of a parent or adult friend, dangle the balloon above a lit lamp bulb.* (It's not necessary to remove the shade.)

*As a safety precaution, never do an experiment using an electric or heat-generating appliance without adult permission and help.

Electricity/Heat

To thoroughly warm the balloon, you'll need to rotate, or turn, the balloon above the bulb for two to three minutes. Then, without removing the balloon from the heat source (you really need an extra hand here), measure the balloon's circumference (widest part) again. Record your information.

What happens:
The balloon measurement is bigger than before!

Why:
When the balloon was heated, the air inside became warmer, causing the air molecules to move faster, bump into each other, and spread out. This action, in turn, increased the size of the balloon.

BLOW-UP: YOU'LL GET A RISE OUT OF IT!

Do the same experiment, but now use new balloons and try new conditions.

Try taping a balloon to a sunny window and measuring it before and after it is exposed to the sun's heat. Also, measure the balloon at different intervals, such as every ten or fifteen minutes. Does the balloon continue to grow larger? How does it change in size, compared to the balloon held over the light bulb?

Remove the balloon from the window until the air inside returns to normal temperature. How long does it take now for the previously expanded now-limp balloon to partially inflate when exposed to the heat?

Spinning Wheel: It's Wheel Science at Work!

Because air molecules expand when heated, the hot air in a hot-air balloon is much lighter than the surrounding air. It's this difference that causes a hot-air balloon to lift off from the ground.

Now you can discover how another gas rises to the occasion to turn a toy's head (a pinwheel, that is).

You need:

aluminum foil circle, 4-to-5-inch (10-13cm) diameter
bendable straw
pot of heated water on stove
sewing needle or pin
scissors
adult help

What to do:

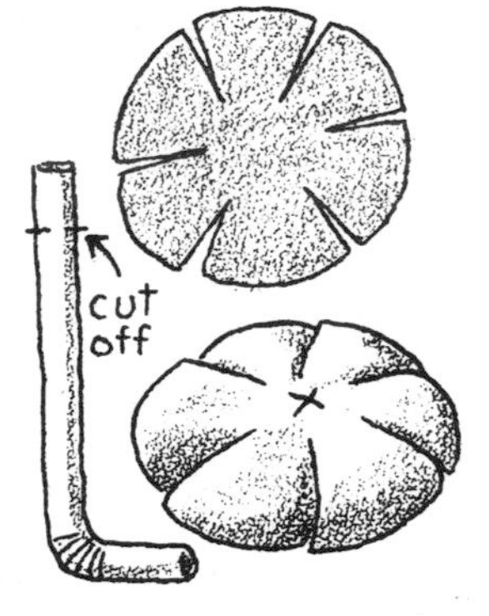

Cut six 1-inch (2.5), equally spaced slits around the aluminum disk or circle. Fold the shiny side down and bend the cut sides downward and back to form vanes or flaps. You should have something that looks like an upside-down pinwheel. Poke a very tiny hole directly in the center of the disk.

Cut a 1-inch (2.5) piece from the bendable straw to use as the balancing piece. Ask your adult helper to poke the needle or pin through the center of the straw, to form a T. The eye or pin head should be sticking out *above* the crossed section.

Now, shiny side down, place the upside-down pinwheel over the eye of the needle. Also, adjust the flaps or vanes of the circle so that they lie smoothly, with a slightly downward bend.

Bend the flexible straw to form a pipe and place the pointed end of the needle into the bent end of the straw.

The next step must be done carefully and with help. Have an adult put about a cup of water in a pot on the stove to heat. When the water begins to simmer and steam, have the adult hold the straw and extend the pinwheel over the very hot water. Watch carefully.

Stove/Steam
Hot water!

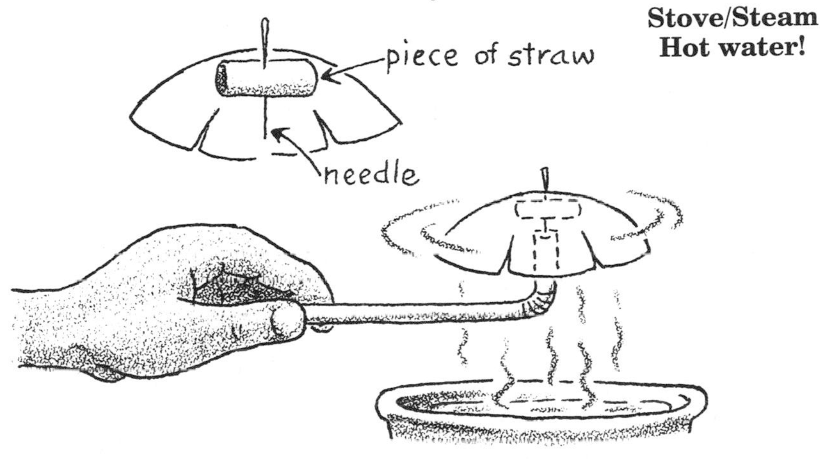

What happens.

The aluminum pinwheel disk gradually and slowly begins to turn.

Why:

Although hot air and steam are not quite the same, they are both gases. Both can "lift" and do work, such as steam engines and hot-air balloons.

The steam here is hot water vapor, a gas. Like hot air, the molecules move faster and take up more space. In turn, they have much energy to move or push an object. Here, the foil pinwheel is turned by the loose, escaping, uprising heated gas molecules.

A MATTER OF GRAVITY

Astronomers, mathematicians, and scientists once believed the planets followed circular paths or orbits around the sun, holding constant speeds as they orbited. Actually, the planets move around the sun in an ellipse, or oval, and according to their distance, or nearness to it and its gravitational pull, they speed up or slow down just enough to keep from being pulled in!

But getting down to Earth! As a resident, your body is being pulled down towards the center of the planet. Your weight on its surface reflects this pull.

In other words, your weight is the result of the pull of Earth's gravity on your body On Mars, your weight would be one-third of your Earth weight, because Mars is smaller. On the moon, with only one-sixth of Earth's gravity, you would weigh even a smaller fraction of your weight on Earth.

Another way of looking at it: the bigger the planet or moon, the more mass and gravity it possesses. So, on larger planets you would weigh more, and on smaller planets you would weigh less.

In this chapter, you'll not only do experiments about the speeds, orbits, and gravity of other planets, but learn how this important force affects our world as well. We know you'll find this chapter very attractive; we're pulling for you!

Curve-Ball Trajectory

Throw a slow or fast ball and watch what kind of curved path, or trajectory, it takes.

You need:
a soft, light ball (for safety)
an assistant (optional), to throw and return ball

What to do:
Throw a ball upward into the air and follow the path, or trajectory, it takes each time you throw it. Repeat the throws, varying or changing the speed of your throw each time; for example, go from slow, to slower, to even slower.

Then, throw some fast balls and notice if the speed has anything to do with changing the curved path the ball takes.

What happens:
All the thrown balls take a curved path once they are released, some following a steeper curve than others.

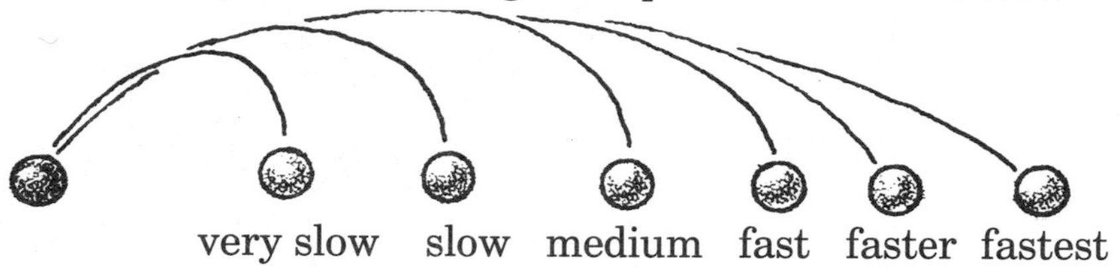

Why:
The balls you threw into the air curved and were pulled back to Earth by its gravitational, or pulling, force. This curved path, the trajectory, in all cases imitates the curvature of the Earth.

When you threw the ball slowly, you could see the curve it took more easily than when the ball was thrown fast. A slower throw, then, will definitely take a steeper, more noticeable path.

Spooling Around

Make a simple twirler, an eraser suspended from a string through a spool, and learn about centripetal force—while spooling around!

You need:

rubber eraser
string, 20 inches (50cm) long
a paper clip
an empty thread spool

What to do:

Tie the string tightly around the eraser and then thread it through the spool. Wrap the other end of the string around the paper clip and tie it securely. The clip will act as the anchor, to stop the string and eraser from flying off.

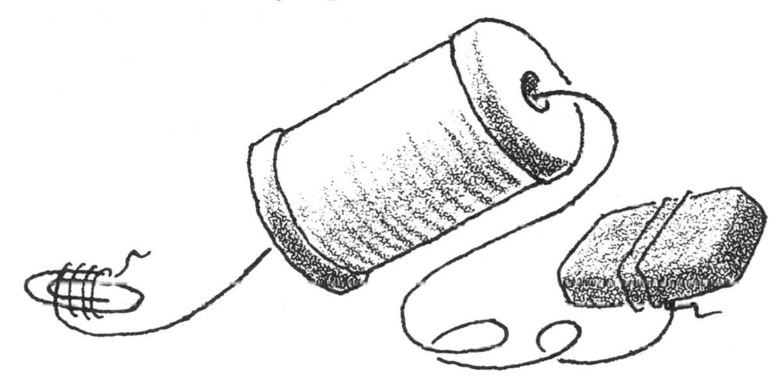

Now you're ready for a test. Hold the twirler straight out, away from your body and above your head. Make sure no one is nearby or in your path.

Watch out!

CAUTION: This experiment involves a whirling object. Do this outside and stay clear of other people.

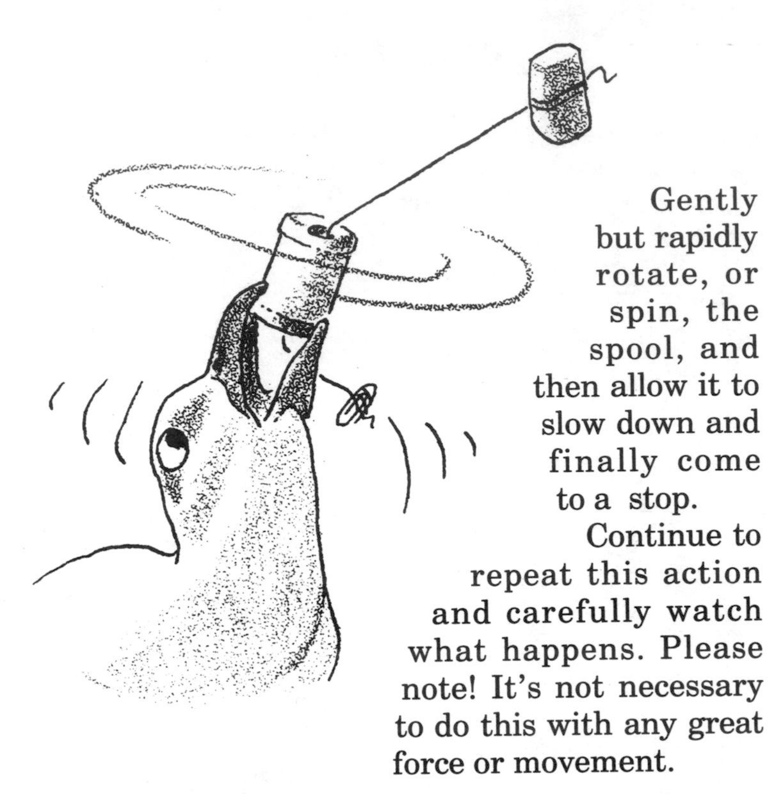

Gently but rapidly rotate, or spin, the spool, and then allow it to slow down and finally come to a stop.

Continue to repeat this action and carefully watch what happens. Please note! It's not necessary to do this with any great force or movement.

What happens:

As you rapidly spin the spool, the eraser will spin away from the spool and will rise upward. When you slow or stop the spinning, the eraser will be pulled downward and eventually stop.

Why:

The eraser on the string is like gravity on the Earth. The string (gravity) pulls the eraser towards it (the spool). What actually is happening is called centripetal force. This is the force that directs movement to the center of the object. When you spun the spool, string, and eraser around you, you pulled the eraser towards you, and the force caused the string and eraser to move up and away from its center.

Weight Lifter: Stringing You Along!

In these whirling experiments you'll use several eraser weights and learn what this tells you about the planets, their gravitational pull, and how they revolve around, or circle, the sun.

So, enjoy twirling and whirling away with no strings attached—well, maybe one!

You need:

5 similar rubber erasers (kneaded or art gum work best)
string, about 40 inches (100cm)
spool
scissors
paper and pencil
an assistant
watch or clock with second hand, or stopwatch

What to do:

As in "Spooling Around," tie one end of the string around an eraser and thread the string through the spool. Tie an eraser to the opposite end of the string. For each trial, you will add one eraser to the bottom of the string. Your assistant's job will be to use the watch or clock to time each 15-second trial and then to record the number of weights and the results.

When you're ready to start each trial, have your helper stand at a distance, ready to start timing. First, get your twirler spinning well, before the official *start* time. Be sure to pull, hold, and keep the bottom-weighted string in the same position for every experiment.

At your start signal, have your helper silently count off 15 seconds as you quietly count the number of turns the eraser makes around the spool before your assistant calls "Time." Report the number of turns to be recorded, then add another eraser—to two, three, then four—and repeat. After each trial, your helper writes down the number of weights used and the number of revolutions, or turns, they make.

What happens:

The more weights or erasers you add to the bottom of your twirler, the more revolutions, or turns, the top one will make in the 15-second allotted time.

Why:

The planets, like Mercury and Venus, that are closest to the sun have to travel faster than those that are at a distance. If these planets did not orbit fast enough, they would be pulled into the sun by its powerful gravitational force.

The twirler with many weights represents the greater gravitational force of the sun on its nearby planets (such as Mercury) and therefore such bodies need to make more revolutions.

However, the sun's gravitational pull on the more distant planets—Uranus, Neptune and Pluto—is much less than on the planets closer to it—Mercury and Venus.

The twirler with one weight (again, the weight represents the gravitational pull of the sun) is like Pluto, with fewer revolutions, or turns, around the sun and, therefore, a smaller number of spins around the spool.

The Big Three: Mercury, Jupiter, Neptune

The next three experiments will strengthen or reinforce what you've learned in "Spooling Around" and "Weight Lifter." You'll more clearly understand the speeds of the orbits of these separate and distantly spaced planets—and if that's not enough, check our chart for planetary rates and see if your numbers and times don't agree with what you already know.

You need:

light cardboard or poster board, at least 22 by 28 inches (56 x 71cm)
a watch with a second hand, or stopwatch
pencil and paper
marbles
scissors
tape

What to do:

Cut three circles from the cardboard, one 10 inches (25.5cm) across, the other 12 inches (30.5cm), the third 14 inches (35.5cm). Next, cut a slit from the outside edge of the circles to the center or middle. Form the circles into cones and tape the outside slits together. Make certain you shape each cone so that the angle or height of the walls is the same. (The trick to doing this accurately and easily is placing the second and third cones inside the first!) When finished, get ready for the fun!

ORBITER I: OPERATION MERCURY

Take the first, the 10-inch, orbiter cone and drop the marble into its center. The center will represent the sun; the marble, Mercury; and the cone, Mercury's orbital path around the sun.

While holding the cone in the palm of your hand, gently rotate or whirl it, keeping the marble orbiting as close to the center as possible without it actually dropping into the center.

Once the marble starts moving in a continuous orbit, with smooth, even rotations or circles, use the watch with the second hand, to time its orbits.

To do this, time and record the number of times the marble makes one full revolution, or circle, in fifteen seconds.

Since Mercury is closest to the sun, our hypothesis, or guess, will state that it will have to move faster around the sun in order to avoid being pulled into it. After you complete the other two experiments, you can chart and compare your results.

ORBITER II: OPERATION JUPITER

Next, place the marble (Jupiter) into the center hole (the sun) of the 12-inch orbital cone. Again, repeat the steps as in "Orbiter I," but this time, whirl or rotate the marble so it makes a wider path or orbit, almost touching the cone's edge. The wider cone represents Jupiter's wider orbit, or path around the sun.

ORBITER III: OPERATION NEPTUNE

Now that you've done the first two experiments, try the third. Yes, you've guessed it! Neptune has a much wider orbit around the sun than the other planets. Use the larger, wider, 14-inch cone for this one. Repeat the steps, but now whirling the marble in a much wider orbit.

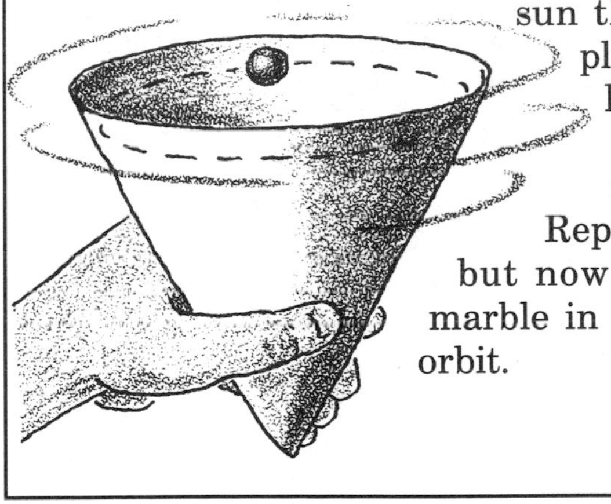

THE BIG THREE: COUNTDOWN!

Using what you already know about the orbits of these three planets, write down or chart your experimental orbital speeds and compare them with our real planetary average estimated speeds.

Mercury speeds around the sun at 108,000 mph. It takes Mercury only 88 Earth days to revolve around the sun.

Jupiter has an average speed around the sun of 29,400 mph. It takes Jupiter practically 12 Earth years to move around the sun.

Neptune's average orbital speed around the sun is 12,200 mph. It takes Neptune over 160 Earth years to travel around the sun.

Is there a connection between your experimental orbital speeds, the distances of orbits from the sun, and the actual estimated speeds of the planets?

To be certain there are no other variables, or things that can change the results, make certain the cones are all evenly smooth circles, and securely taped. For best test results, do at least three or four such trials and compare them to the actual estimates.

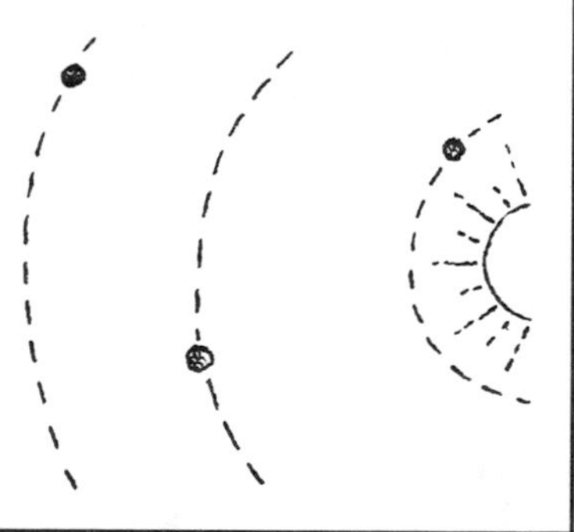

I Get Around

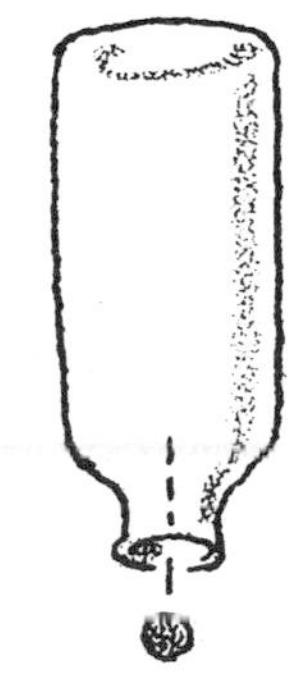

A marble's in a bottle The bottle is turned upside down. The marble stays inside! How? A full-of-surprises trick that will have your friends standing on *their* heads.

You need:

plastic 2-liter bottle   small marble

What to do:

Drop the marble in the bottle and ask your friends if they can turn the bottle upside down without having the marble drop out. And "No," they can't simply hold the marble inside!

"Impossible," they say. Now it's your turn. Holding the bottle upright, with your hand underneath, move the bottle to start the marble whirling in a circular orbit within it. While continuing to swirl the bottle and the marble within, gradually move the bottle to a horizontal and then to an upside-down position.

What happens:

The revolving whirling marble doesn't fall out of the bottle, even when the bottle is turned upside down.

Why:

When your friends simply turned the bottle, not whirling it, the Earth's gravity pulled the marble down and out. However, by whirling the bottle, the marble was pulled up away from the neck to the side of the bottle by centrifugal force.

Slam Dunk

Gravity is a lot like a slam dunk, pushing a basketball forcefully down through a hoop. But gravity's force pushes *everything* down. In order to fly, an airplane's lift must be greater than the downward pull of gravity. Show that gravity is a *persistent* force; the results are the same, even if we try to change them.

You need:

a large hardbound book
table
2 rulers
2 coins

What to do:

Place the book on the table so one end hangs off the end. Place a ruler about an inch (2cm) away from the book, with an end hanging over it. Place one coin on the end of the extended part of the ruler; the other, at the top of the end of the book in the space next to the ruler. Now, use the other ruler to forcefully strike the end of the extended, overhanging ruler so that both coins are pushed to the ground.

Will forcefully pushing the ruler to the side to hit one of the coins greatly affect its fall? Which coin will hit the floor first?

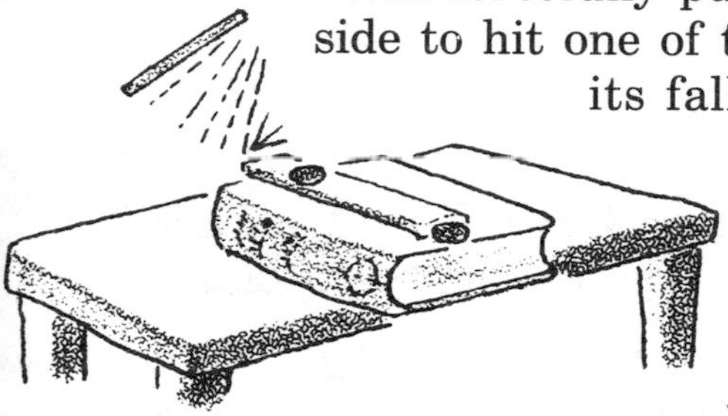

What happens:

Both coins hit the floor at the same time.

Why:

The force of gravity is always the same. In our experiment, a forceful side hit to the coin by the ruler was greater than the force that caused the coin to drop off its extended end. However, even this effect was not enough to alter or change the rate of fall.

Gumdrop

Will a large art gum eraser hit the floor before a small paper clip? What about a flat sheet of paper or aluminum foil? Does size, shape, and weight affect the rate of fall, or how fast an object falls to Earth? Try these experiments, by gum, and erase all doubt!

You need:

scissors
sheet of paper
sheet of aluminum foil
art gum eraser, or
object equal in size
paper clip

What to do:

With an aluminum foil sheet laying on one hand, and a paper sheet on the other, extend your arms. Drop both sheets at the same time and observe what happens.

Now repeat the experiment, but replace one sheet with a eraser. Follow this by dropping the paper clip and a sheet. Last, drop the eraser and paper clip at the same time.

What happens:

The paper and the foil, in general, float down to the floor at the same rate, while the eraser and the paper clip hit the floor before either the foil or the paper sheet. Finally, both the eraser and paper clip hit the floor at the same time.

Why:

The size and the weight of the clip and eraser do not affect the rate of fall. This is because most of their mass is inside. The amount of metal and eraser forming their surface areas is small, so drag from air resistance is reduced. Gravity pulls on both objects with the same equal force, ounce for ounce.

However, the flat sheets of paper and foil, with their masses spread out over a wider surface area, met much more air resistance. It was this greater drag that affected their rate of fall.

THE SKY IS FALLING

Let's take the last two experiments, "Slam Dunk" and "Gumdrop," a step further. Take a few much heavier objects and some that are very lightweight. Again, in pairs, hold them out at the same height, or level, and drop them. Do both hit the floor at the same time? Do some hit sooner?

Now try a similar, but different, experiment. Take two matching round toy balloons (same kind and size, but color doesn't matter). Blow up one balloon until it is the size of a large cantaloupe, and knot it closed. Hold the balloons by the necks, the inflated balloon in one hand and the deflated (not blown up) balloon in the other. Make certain the two balloons are held out at equal height, then drop them at the same time. Which balloon hits the ground first?

Try holding the deflated balloon much higher than the inflated balloon. Is there any difference in the drop, or is it the same? Why are the results with the falling balloons different from the other objects that were dropped?

Using what you already know about flight, gravity, air, drag, airfoils, and other experiments, how do you explain the results you got with this experiment?

Balance Beam & Airheads

Here we'll stretch one experiment into two. First, you'll find the center of gravity in "Balance Beam," and then the "Airheads" will show you their stuff.

You need:

¼-inch (0.5cm) diameter dowel
overhead fixture, from which to hang dowel
string
4 balloons
safety pin

For Balance Beam:

Loosely tie one end of a long piece of string to something high up and let the string hang down. Tie the dowel to the other end of it.

Yes! That's right! All you have to do for this experiment is simply adjust the dowel on the string so that it is perfectly balanced. In other words, find the dowel's center of gravity, the point on the dowel where its weight, or mass, is centered. At this point, the dowel will be balanced on the string, and will hang there horizonally. You'll find the dowel's center of gravity somewhere in the middle of it.

For Airheads:

Cut four more 15-inch (40cm) strings. Tie and space two on one side of the dowel and two on the other.

Inflate the four balloons equally. Knot the necks or tie the openings tightly with string, then tie each balloon onto one of the four separate strings on the dowel. The balloons should be equally spaced and the dowel's center of gravity balanced.

With the safety pin, pop one of the balloons. Adjust the dowel's center of gravity. Pop a second balloon. Now, with only two balloons remaining, readjust the balance and pop one of the last remaining balloons

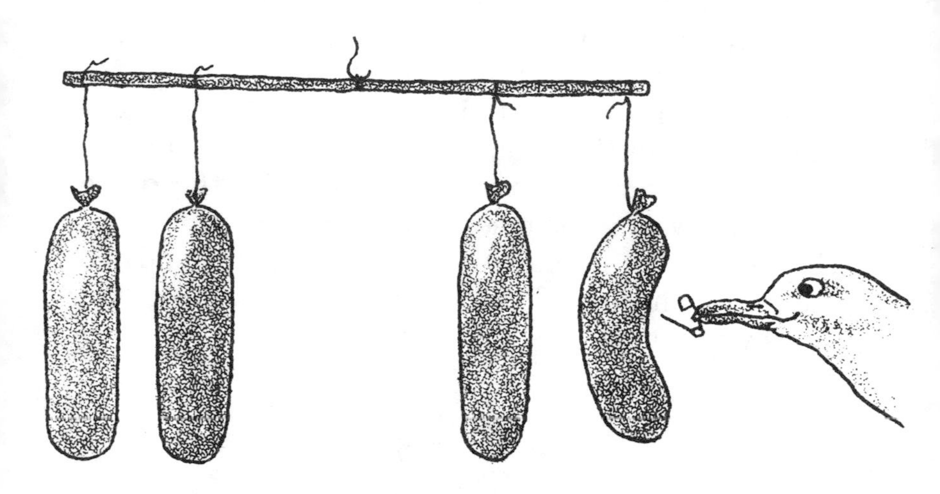

When you popped one of the two remaining balloons, the dowel, and the one remaining balloon, dropped and fell to one side.

This proves you should never take air lightly. It has weight and it is heavy—it's definitely a weighty subject!

FLYPAPER

A long time ago, someone took a sheet of paper, folded it, aimed it, and threw it. It became the first flying paper, or glider.

Here's your chance to build an assortment of gliders and, in the interest of science, your teacher or parents can't really complain. You'll find out which materials are best to use, what designs fly best, and which attachments or parts make a difference to flight.

Now, get ready to build gliders with different designs, parts, and with ailerons, or flaps—and prepare to soar.

Flight: Still Up in the Air?

Still confused about the ups and downs of flight? No problem. We'll start out working with a basic glider and add or take away "extras," the variables, that make your plane fly great, good, well... Well, maybe not so well! But you'll be air-minded in no time.

You need:

sheet of paper
measuring tape or stick

What to do:

Fold the paper in half lengthwise and crease (1). Open the fold, and fold the two corners at one end in towards the center line (2). Crease at the fold.

Now, bring each of the two folded edges of the triangle to the center line. Align the folds against the center line, and crease the new folds (3).

Finally, turning the glider, align one fold against the center line and crease. Then do the same on the opposite side (4). Hold the glider up and position the wings outward (5). If done correctly, the nose tip of the glider should point slightly downward.

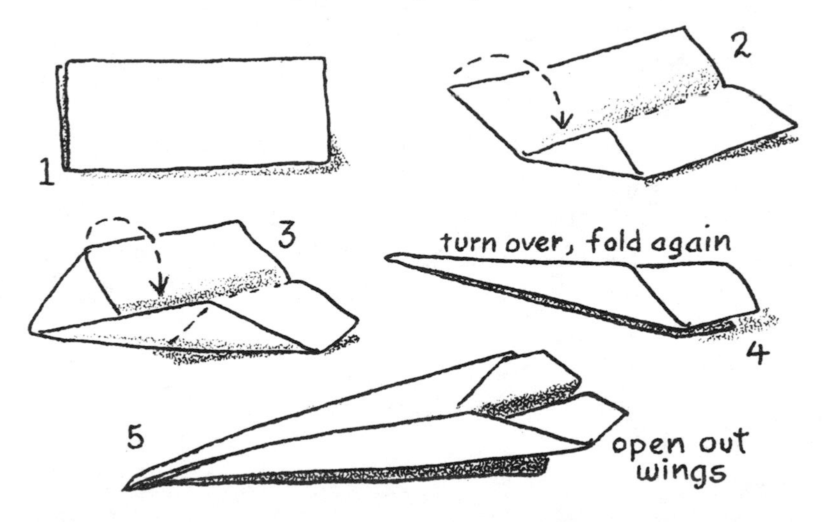

You are now ready to test your craft. It should be thrown each time by the same person and in the same way. After each throw, the distance traveled should be carefully measured and noted.

What happens:

With each throw, your glider should soar, circle, swoop, or descend swiftly, traveling a good distance.

Why:

Your glider is an excellent example of an airfoil. If you examine the wings, you'll notice they curve slightly on the top and are flat on the bottom. The air passing over the top of the wing is forced to travel faster, due to the raised shape, and the faster air becomes thinner than the air passing under the wing.

Because the air underneath is denser, or thicker—because it is traveling more slowly—the denser air pushes the plane upward, into the thinner air. It is this process, or law of nature on air movement, that keeps your glider soaring aloft, or in flight.

AIRLINES

A glider's flight depends on its lines, or shape, and how it is designed. Try using different sizes or weights of paper. Fold some lengthwise, others by width. Which work best? Make gliders with wider wings or longer noses, always testing each separately and keeping other variables the same. Keep track of the results (smoothness of flight, distance traveled) and the differences in the planes.

CLIPPED WINGS

Flaps or clips, which do you prefer? Maybe both? Try flight experiments with paper clips placed in different places on the planes to stabilize them, or make them fly steadier and straighter.

Fly each separate design against your basic, no-frills model. In each case, test the distance traveled and the smoothness of flight. For example, test the basic plane against one that has a clip on the end of each wing, then test another design, and so on. This example of experimentation, comparing a basic model against one that has been altered or changed in one way, is called *controlled*.

You can also try taping the wings of one model together, cutting adjustable flaps in each wing-ending of another, or attaching a rudder, or tail, to a third.

There are countless combinations or possibilities—try them all or just a few. After you have thoroughly experimented with your altered or changed models and compared them with the basic glider, form a hypothesis, or guess, on why some models fly better than others. Can you now test out your hypothesis?

With each test, keep accurate and careful records: distances traveled, smoothness of flight, less than successful landings. Remember, you can learn more from mistakes and failures than from smooth sailing. Every obstacle provides an opportunity to learn. By making and flying gliders, you can learn a lot about flight.

KITE TALES

Once upon a time in the land of Woo, a Chinese province, a man named Sun-Wing was very lonely. Waion, the god of the wind, was very lonely too.

To please Waion, Sun-Wing tied and placed two thin birch sticks across very thin paper and then attached it to a cord. Sun-Wing let Waion catch his paper windbird and lift it on high. Suddenly, both Sun-Wing and Waion realized they were no longer lonely. On Waion's command, the paper wind bird danced, glided, swooped, and dived.

You, too, can make your own paper windbird and, under Waion's command, maybe it, too, will dance, glide, swoop, and dive.

Our Fantastic Mini Box Kite

Our mini box kite is fun to make and fly, and you only need a few simple materials. You'll need, too, some measuring skills, but not to worry—it's all here in black and white. We won't leave you up in the air—but the kite will.

You need:

sheet of paper	scissors	hole punch or nail
ruler	tape	string

What to do:

On the paper, measure and draw a 6½ by 8-inch (17 ×20cm) rectangle. Cut the rectangle out, then fold it in half, and crease. Next, open it and fold in each end of the sheet to the center line and crease again. Open and you have the makings of an open-ended box shape with sides measuring 2 inches (5cm).

Now, you need to make four fairly equal rectangular "windows" in each of the four box sides. To do this, flatten the sheet, lay a ruler against the inner side of each crease, and draw lines across, to help guide you. Now, 3/8 inch (1cm) in from each guide line and ¾ inch (2cm) in from each edge of the paper, draw the 1¼ by 5-inch (3×13cm) windows in each side. Lay the ruler across the windows to check that they align and are centered; then cut them out.

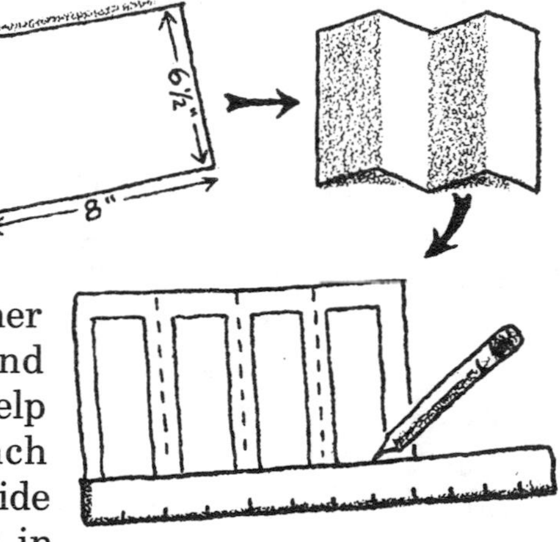

Next, tape the two end sides of the rectangular box neatly together, and you have a mini box kite. To prepare it for flight, carefully make two small holes, or use tape, and attach a string bridle. Then fly! It's easy as a breeze!

A real, old-time box kite looks more like the one shown at left. Using straws and long strips of lightweight paper, why not try making a small model and see if it flies. Then, you can try toothpicks and smaller strips of tissue paper for an even smaller version! Where will it all end?

CAUTION: Kites must only be flown in an open area or field, *never* near electrical power lines.

Power lines!

BOX KITE BRIDLE

Tie a string 12 inches (30 cm) long to equal ends of the kite, leaving enough slack or sag in the middle to attach the kite string. Tie a 2 to 3 yard or meter length of string about 2 inches (5 cm) down from one end of the bridle. Later, you can add more string if you wish.

Build a Simple Kite! It's a Breeze!

Get the family together for this high-flying fun! Kitemaking is an "exact" science and an art involving designing work, stringing, framing, and bridle, so it's nice to have adult help.

You can learn a lot about the principles of aerodynamics when you build and fly one of the earliest and oldest flying toys and machines, the ever-fantastic kite!

You need:

two ¼-inch (0.5cm) diameter dowels:
one 30 inches (75cm) long and
one 28 inches (70cm) long
tool for cutting and notching dowels
a large work area
newspapers
tissue paper
scissors
string
tape
glue
measuring stick or tape
pencil
adult assistant

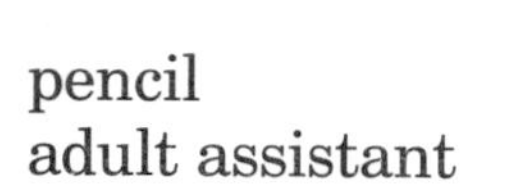

Sharp tool!

What to do:

Ask an adult to cut small grooves or notches on the ends of each wooden dowel or stick. String will be run through these slits to make the frame, so the notches need to be deep enough to hold it.

Find the middle of your 28-inch (70cm) cross stick—14 inches (35cm) in from the ends. Mark it.

Next, mark a place on the upright main, or mast, stick 8 inches (20cm) from one end. Placed toward the top, this is the point where the two sticks will meet to form a cross. Using a figure-8 wrap, fix the two sticks together carefully with string until they are fastened.

Work a long piece of string into the end notches of each dowel as you form the frame of the kite. Pull the string slightly to tighten it around the frame, then tie it off.

You will probably need two sheets of tissue paper to form the skin, or sail, of the kite. If so, lay one tissue paper sheet over the other, leaving a 1-inch (2.5cm) margin overlap. Carefully tape the sheets along the seam, both front and back.

Lay the kite frame on the tissue paper. Leave an edging of at least 2 inches (5cm) of paper to fold and glue down. Cut around the frame as shown.

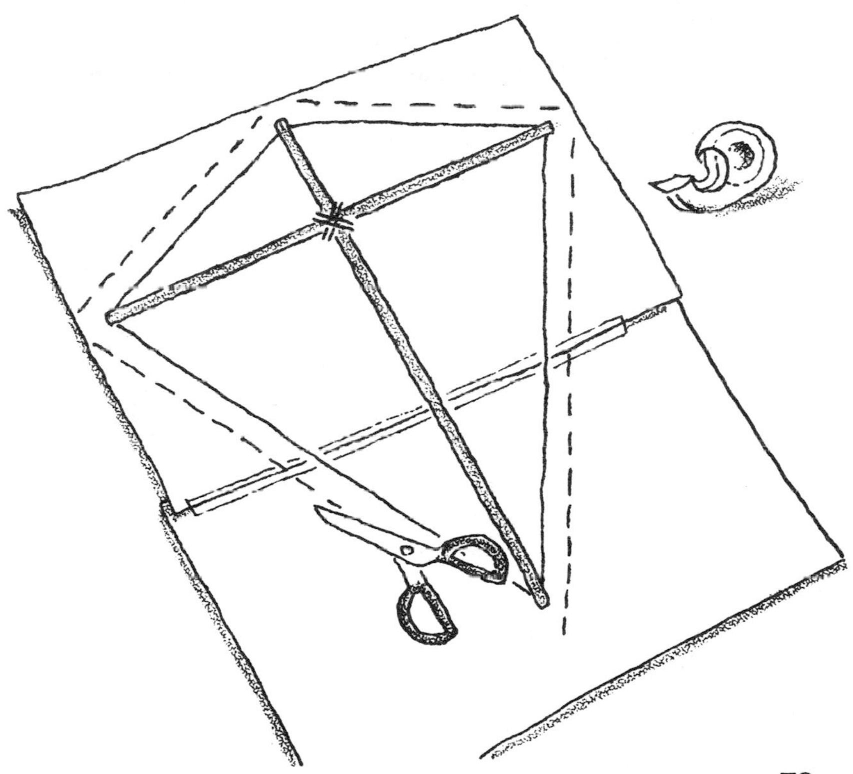

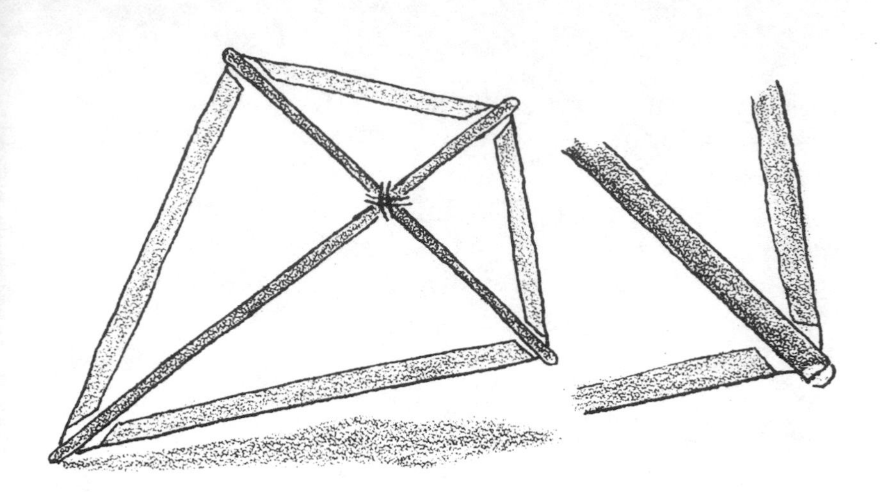

When finished, glue the overlap, or end, flaps (a glue stick works well) down over the string frame. Keep your scissors handy. It's important to trim away extra paper so that the end sticks are free and clear. Also, pull the tissue slightly so that it is taut on the frame, but be careful not to to rip the paper.

What happens:

If all the variables are right (kite construction, bridle, tail, wind direction and speed), your kite should be lifted up high into the air and stay there, dancing against the sky.

Why:

The action of air lifting a kite is similar to that of an airfoil or an airplane wing. The air flowing over it has a longer way to go and has less force than the air against its near surface. As a result, the air pressure exerts a greater force on the front of the kite than on its back and the kite is pulled up, up, and away!

The string you pull towards you, on the other hand, holds and steadies the kite, balancing it in the air.

Hightail It to the Bridle Party

Let this be a family project—a bridle party and a kite launching. Your tail and bridle, the string harness attached to the main or flying string on your kite, needs to be made and attached carefully—and with your aerodynamic mind, you should be highly successful.

To make a bridle, or kite harness, attach a long string to the ends of the upright stick. The string should be slack, or loose, enough so it pulls out.

Next, attach a shorter string to the ends of the dowel that make up the cross stick and make them meet a little below it. Adjust the bridle strings so they are equal and tight, and tie the flying string to where the bridle strings meet.

At this point, it's important to test your kite to see if it "catches the wind" properly—if not, it will not fly at all or will fly incorrectly. With the bridle

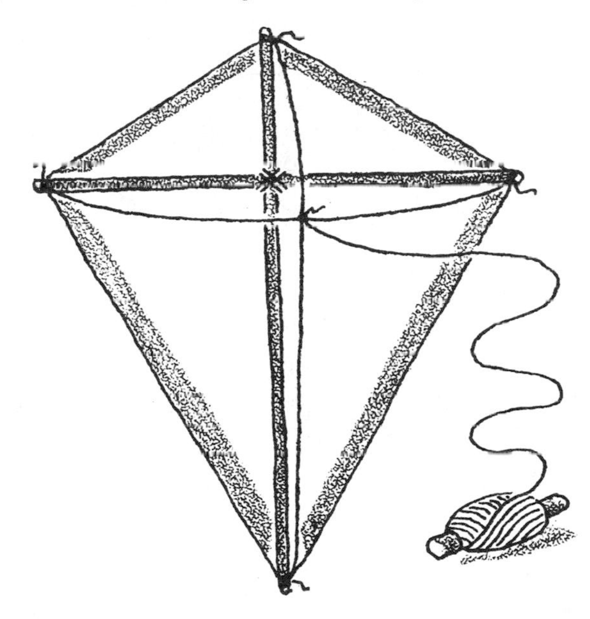

and flying string attached, stand in the wind and pull the kite towards you. If the top of the kite pulls upward and the kite tilts and seems to be gathering-in the wind, your bridle is correctly attached. If this is not the case, adjust the cross string to a higher or lower position and try again.

To add a tail (to help balance the kite), cut rectangular pieces of colored tissue (multi-colored or a variety of colored pieces show up best). Space and tie them, using smaller pieces of string, every 7 to 8 inches (18–20cm) along a 6 to 8-foot (2–3m) tail string.

Tie the tail to the bottom end of the upright stick and get ready to soar—and have a high-falutin', high-flyin' time!

OTHER IDEAS BLOWING IN THE WIND

Now that you've put together your first basic kite, why not try building other kites (maybe a six-cornered face kite or a bird-star kite). With a few more dowels and a lot of imagination, you can expand on the directions for building your basic model. Also, you can decorate your model with marker pens, pasted-on bright tissue panels, a variety of exciting shapes, and streamers—with all you know and all you can do, the sky's the limit!

EXPLORATION IN OUTER SPACE?

OUT OF THIS WORLD!

From *Skylab* (the American space station put into orbit in 1973) to the space shuttle *Endeavor*, launched in 1993, and to recent cooperative efforts in the long-lasting Russian *Mir*, as well as Pathfinder's "invasion" of Mars, space exploration has never been more exciting.

In this chapter, you'll do experiments that teach you about the conditions in outer space, watch the reentry of a space capsule, make your own space food, and even design a space station and man it.

Too, you'll create conditions and craters on the moon and design logo space patches for imaginative and creative fun. So, get ready to blast-off for an out-of-this-world adventure!

SIGNS FROM SPACE: AN

Astronauts often wear specially designed emblems, known as patches, on their clothing to indicate their unit and tell, in pictures and words, something about the unit's mission in space. The Gemini and Apollo crew members wore such patches on their sleeves, and future astronauts will certainly wear their own similar emblems proudly.

You can design your own emblem, or badge, simply and easily. First, pick up some heavy tagboard—sold at stationery and variety stores, art supply or drugstores. Use your imagination and brightly colored markers, crayons, or pencils, as well as creative lettering and a variety of space scenes, to turn out exciting, creative crew badges.

How about a space scene, circling suns, or draw some alien terrain or ground surface. Will your badge-emblem show a

EMBLEMATIC CONCERN

planet with several moons, or a landscape with huge craters, deep surface cracks, or volcanoes? Will you have a rocket on your badge or a futuristic space shuttle or space station? The possibilities are endless, and with ideas all around you, you'll have no problem getting started.

Give your pretend outer-space mission a name—remember the *Discovery* and *Columbia* missions?—and include your own mission name on your badge. Use imaginative lettering for an extra-special effect. Select an interesting shape—square, triangle, circle, oval, or maybe a shield—for each badge. When you finish your emblem, cut out the shape and attach a small safety pin to the backside of each badge, using small precut strips of masking tape. Now, your crew is ready to explore flight and space and to let their imaginations soar.

Reentry Splashdown

Ever wonder how early astronauts, before shuttles, got back to Earth after rocketing into space? This simple experiment, using only a few simple, easy-to-find materials, will show you how it was done.

You need:

1 fast-food beverage cup
a paper towel sheet
string, about 80 inches (200cm)
4 12-inch (30cm) lengths of string
eraser
tape
hole punch
scissors

What to do:

Cut away the top of a throwaway cup, leaving only a 2-inch-deep bottom portion. With the hole punch, make a hole about ½ inch (1cm) from the top of the cup and tie the long string to the cup.

Next, assemble the parachute and space capsule portion of the experiment. To do this, tape the four 12-inch (30cm) strings to each corner of the paper towel. Gather the other ends of the strings together and tie them around the eraser. Test your parachute-capsule. Try balling it up in your hand and tossing it into the air a few times. The parachute should open easily and be balanced to float the eraser to the ground.

Now, to demonstrate how an orbiting space-capsule reenters Earth's atmosphere, take all your experimental props (chute-capsule and beverage cup) outside. You'll need room to whirl your space capsule over your head without worrying about it hitting things or someone nearby.

Place the eraser in the bottom of the cup. Gently pack the paper chute on top of the eraser. Don't stuff it all the way down into the cup. It is easier to do the forced reentry simulation if it is loosely packed.

Now, find a clear spot outside and begin whirling your space capsule overhead. Start slowly, and gradually increase the speed. The parachute will stay in place in the cup as long as you continue to whirl it smoothly. Now, slow the whirling motion and purposely jerk the string sharply. You may have to do this several times and in different ways before you get the hang of ejecting the parachute-capsule.

Always remember that scientists often try many different ways of doing something before they find not only an acceptable but the best way or answer. If, after several tries, your capsule does not eject or the parachute does not open properly, check the weight of your eraser, how it fits the cup—maybe too tightly?—and readjust and repack the parachute.

What happens:

After you slow the whirling motion and jerk on the string, the parachute and capsule eject, or pop out of the cup. The chute opens and floats the capsule easily and gently to the ground.

Why:

You have demonstrated how space capsules used to be recovered or brought back from Earth's orbit and made a soft landing. The slowing of the whirling motion and the jerking of the string represented the firing of retrorockets that slowed the capsule's forward motion so that gravity would pull it towards Earth.

The string represents the balance of gravity and centrifugal force that kept space capsules in orbit so they would not fly out into space. The space capsule's orbit was similar to your turning and whirling the string-cup parachute.

To prepare for and deploy your parachute capsule for reentry, you slowed the whirling motion and jerked the string. This was like firing retrorockets and, once a space capsule reached Earth's atmosphere, the parachute automatically opened to float the capsule to Earth.

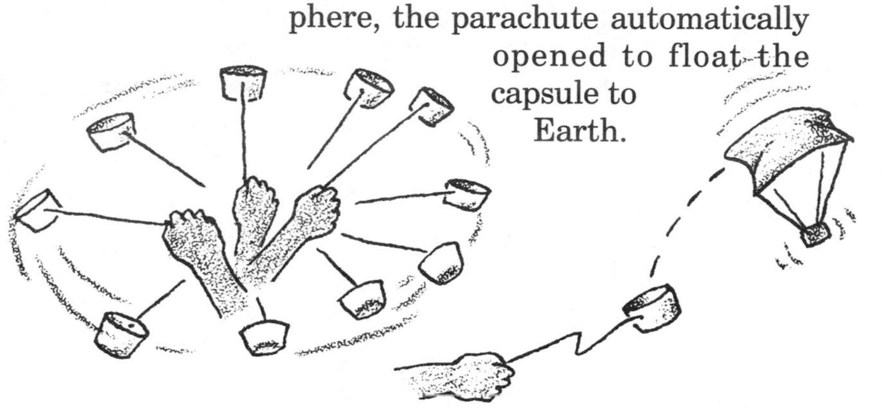

The space capsule landings were made at sea—called "splashdowns"! Today, astronauts travel into space in modern spacecrafts, called shuttles. They are pushed into orbit by orbiter and booster rockets that return to Earth, where they are recovered and reused. Astronauts now fly their shuttlecraft back to Earth like planes, to be used again and again, unlike space capsules. Some early capsules that were saved and studied after splashdown are on display in space museums.

Moonscape I: Mark-It-Research

To see close up, and even touch the moon, make your very own model moonscape. It's easy, and you'll find out how some lunar features, or surface marks, were formed. As a bonus, you can name craters, mountains, and seas on your moonscape after anyone you want!

You need:

½ cup plaster of paris
½ cup boiling water
shallow, flat frozen food or aluminum pan
adult help
plastic spoon or other throw-away utensil
magnifying hand lens

What to do:

While a parent or adult brings the one-half cup of water to a rolling boil on the stove, pour the half cup of plaster of paris over the bottom of the pan.

Hot water!

Have your helper pour about half of the very hot water *carefully* into the pan. Stir it briefly to moisten all the plaster. If needed, add more of the water to dry sections. Don't worry about a few lumps. They're meant for great things!

When the mixture cools a bit, becoming partially solid, pour off any excess water. Place the pan where it can be left undisturbed for about an hour to dry.

After the plaster mix has completely dried, take your model moonscape and observe its features, the surface areas, with a magnifying glass. Map out and pencil in names and areas on your model; name the seas, or *maria*; the rougher, patchy areas; the mountains; lumpy areas; and the craters, those different-sized holes you find. Look at the moonscape in the early-morning or late-afternoon sunshine, or use a flashlight, to see how the different features cast shadows on the moonscape.

What happens:

As the plaster of paris hardens, the lumpier areas grow in size to form mountains; holes of various sizes appear in the surface to form craters; and rough, flat surfaces become the seas or plains.

Why:

Billions of impact holes or craters cover all of the moon's surface, the mountainous areas as well as the flat sea, or plains, areas known as maria. These "seas" (not bodies of water at all but wide areas of volcanic rock) were formed billions of years ago as the flowing hot lunar surface cooled.

Evidence from the Apollo explorations and moon landings have proven that many lunar features or surface marks were caused by underground forces as the moon's molten and hot liquid center cooled, deep beneath the hardened crust.

When our hot plaster mixture cools, as the surface of the moon did long ago, it also forms craters, rough areas, and large lumpy, mountainous areas. These features are due, again, to the heating and cooling of the surface, the contraction or shortening, and the expansion or lengthening of its crust.

METEORS!

However, most of the holes, or craters, on the moon's surface were formed by meteorites. Chunks of space rock have been striking the lunar surface for many thousands of years. Since the moon has no air clinging to it, those space rocks, or meteors, do not burn up in the atmosphere, like most of those that fall towards Earth. And, without water or wind to smooth the lunar surface roughness, craters upon craters form a history of the surface impacts.

Moonscape II: A Heavy Hitter!

Go one step further and find out how the size of asteroids and the falling speed of meteorites can affect the size and depth of moon craters. Careful, this is a messy experiment! Do it outside, wear old clothes, and put newspapers under your experiment pan to make it easy to clean up your mess when you're done.

You need:

- small, flat container (disposable pan or tray)
- "meteors"—small ball, large marble, lumps of clay, stones
- 1 cup flour, baking soda, or fine sand
- ruler or measuring stick
- pencil and paper
- newspaper

What to do:

Place the cup of flour, baking soda, or sand in the container. Mound it first into a hill in one corner of the tray, then level it down, smoothing it off with your hand from that corner to the others. This will represent the surface of the moon.

Next, take the "meteor" and drop it from 4 to 5 inches (10–13cm) above the filled tray surface. Measure the hole, or crater, the dropped item made in the powdery surface; the distance across from one crater wall to the other; and the depth of the hole. Record the height of the "meteor" fall, from where you dropped it to the surface in the tray, and the measurements of the crater it made. Draw pictures and put the measurements in as labels.

After each trial drop, smooth off the surface powder and try again. Double the distance of your last drop, or gradually increase the height of your drops. Each time, use the meter or yardstick to measure the drop heights and the ruler to find the diameters of the craters made by the impacts. Keep good records and illustrations.

According to your notes and measurements, what did you observe between greater-distance drops and closer-distance ones?

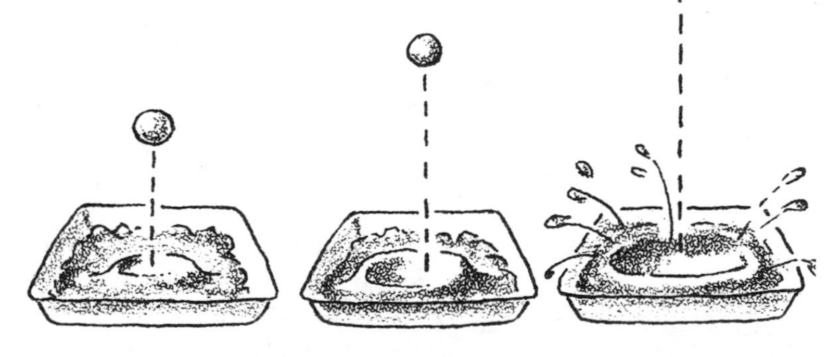

CREATIVE CRATERS

Now that you're an expert at creating craters and measuring them, try including a few variables, or other things that could affect moon crater size.

Try dropping different-sized spheres at different heights and compare them to your original or first drops. Also, try "throwing" some down onto the surface, not just dropping them. Will the impact, or hit, be greater and so produce a larger crater? Again, like a good scientist, be patient, keep good notes and records, and compare many different things.

After all your experiments, what can you decide about the cause of crater size on the moon?

Moonscape III: Making a Good Impression

Simulate or copy the conditions on the moon and Earth and then compare each. Unlike the Earth, the moon has little or no erosion or surface breakdown. A crater, footprint, or any other impression or mark on the surface could last for millions of years!

You need:

- an undisturbed outdoor location; optional: outdoor tool shed or cabinet
- 2 small disposable dishes (plastic or aluminum trays or dishes work well)
- corrugated shallow box lid
- object to make a good print or impression in the soil

trowel or spoon for mixing
pencil and paper
1 cup soil
2 cups sand (bagged sand can be found in garden sections of drugstores or variety stores)

What to do:
Fill each container with ½ cup of soil and 1 cup of sand. Mix each well with a trowel or spoon.

Press the imprinting object firmly into each surface. If the print does not come out well, smooth over the surface and try again.

Place one of the trays in an undisturbed location and label it *Earthscape*. Also write Day One and the date.

For clearest test results, place the exposed "Earth" sample in an unprotected, open area where wind, rain, and other elements can do their work.

Place the other dish, labeled *Moonscape,* in an additional undisturbed location. Also, place the box lid over the dish and weight it with a heavy object. Better yet, if an outdoor cabinet or shed is available, use it to enclose your *moon sample*, with or without the lid.

Again, label the experiment as you did in the *Earthscape* sample. Observe each sample over a 7–14 day period and write down what you see.

What happens:

The experiment tray left outside unprotected soon is broken down; it wears away until little or any of the original print or impression is left.

The experiment dish covered with the box lid and/or in the closet remains as it was originally. There is little erosion and the impression or print remains clear.

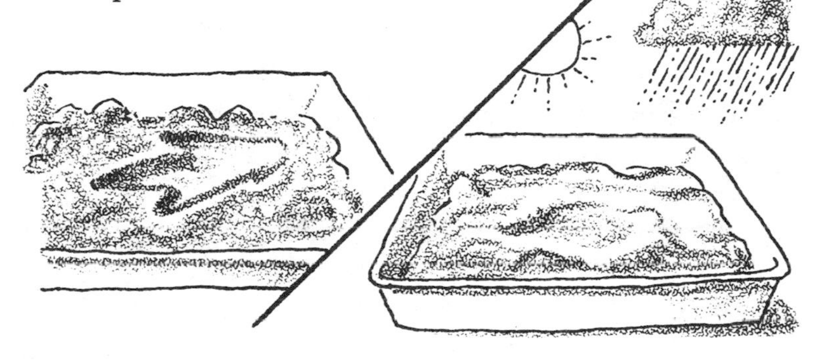

Why:

Since the moon has no atmosphere, there is no wind, water, rain, and snow or other atmospheric elements that would cause surface breakdown, or erosion. This, too, is somewhat like our protected experiment.

When comets, asteroids, and meteors hit the lunar surface, there is no weathering force to affect the impact or craters they form.

The Earth's atmospheric conditions, however, produce wind, water, rain, and snow. These same conditions, similar to our exposed experiment, cause weathering and erosion, or a natural wearing away of rocks and soil.

Moving Picture

Since the moon revolves or moves around the Earth, how does a spacecraft going to the moon hit its moving target?

Find a couple of friends and try this fun demonstration. It definitely will move you to think.

You need:

3 or more people
watch with a second hand (or stopwatch)
paper and pencil
a large open field or place to run (the school track would be great)

What to do:

Mark off a large circular running area or arrange to use a school track.

Have someone time how long it takes a runner to go around the large outside track once at a constant rate of speed. Record the time. Have a second runner run a smaller circular track within the larger track. Again have someone time this runner and record the results.

Now, start both runners running their tracks at their same rates of speed. When ready, or at your

signal, the runner moving on the inner track should gradually and steadily increase the diameter of the running circle in order to join up with the runner on the outer track.

Again, the person with the stopwatch should record the time it takes for the inner runner to join the outside runner.

What happens:

The inside runner has a hard time trying to join up with the runner on the outer track, likely having to speed up or slow down to do it.

Why:

In order for a spacecraft to intersect the moon, timing is very important. Calculations are made before launch so that fuel is not wasted in slowing down, speeding up, or changing course in flight. The speeds of both the craft and the moon have to be taken into account, and also the speed necessary for the craft to overcome the force of Earth's gravity. Actually, to "catch" the moon, the spacecraft must be directed ahead of it, where the moon *will be*. Now have your runners try joining up again and see if they can better their time.

PLAN-IT!

Plan a diagram or chart of the inner planets, showing their orbits and sizes. It's simple and easy and we'll show you how.

Find a cleared desk or table for a workspace. First, you'll need an inexpensive pencil compass for making circles For additional accuracy, an inexpensive circle stencil or template, showing the diameter of circles, can be bought at the same store. However, if you insist on drawing freehand, that's okay with us too! We'll describe each planet's size and orbit and even give you a few helpful and needed suggestions.

Finally, you'll need a standard sheet of paper. For a bonus effect, you can use colored markers, pencils, crayons, or colored construction paper.

Our sun is about 865,000,000 miles in diameter (almost 1,400,000 kilometers across). One hundred Earths could fit inside the sun.

Draw a circle in the middle of your paper about the size of a quarter. If you're using a stencil, a 5/16-inch circle will do. If you wish, you can decorate your sun with flame-like spokes to represent the sun's outer area, or corona.

Next, set your compass to the ¾-inch (2cm) mark and place its point in the middle of the sun. Carefully move the paper or the pencil around so the compass pencil-point marks the paper. (Helpful hint: Holding the center pointer down as you move the pencil around will help prevent skipping or moving.) This circle represents Mercury's orbit around the sun.

Place a pea-size circle on this path or 3/16 inch on the stencil (Mercury). Actually, next to our sun, Mercury is merely a grain of sand. Mercury is only about 3,030 miles wide and is 36,000,000 miles or (58,000,000km) away from the sun.

Position your compass on 1½ inch (4cm) for Venus' orbit and follow the same marking procedure as you did with Mercury's orbit. Venus' path around the sun is over 67,000,000 miles (about 108,000,000km) from the sun. Nearly Earth size, it is about 7,500 miles across (about 12,000km). Draw a circle on the orbit about the size of a large pea or a ¼-inch (0.8cm) circle on the stencil.

Our planet Earth comes next. Set your compass to the 2 inch (5cm) mark and follow the marking procedure for the other orbits. Since Venus and Earth are close to the same size, use the same circle for Earth as you did for Venus. Our Earth is

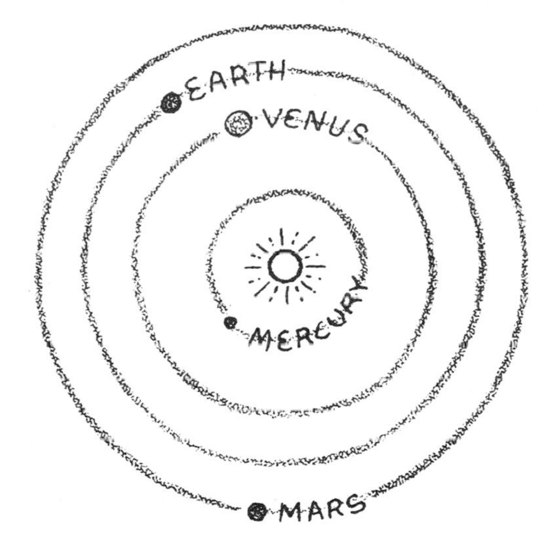

just under 8,000 miles in diameter (7,927 actually, about 12,757km). It is about 93,000,000 miles from the sun, or about 150,000,000km.

The last inner planet is Mars. According to its orbits, it's at least 50,000,000 miles away from Earth, 142,000,000 miles away from the sun and over 4,000 miles wide (over 6,700km). Use a 6.5cm setting on your compass for an orbit and a slightly smaller size than Earth or Venus for the diameter, or width, of this planet. For continuation with the outer planets, see "Plan-It Plus!"

PLAN-IT PLUS!

Now that you've mastered the compass and distances of inner planets and sizes, why not do a large diagram of all the planets. You'll need a large white poster board and some information on the outer planets.

With the information provided below, you can mathematically calculate, or figure out, the scaled distances of orbits and the sizes of the outer planets.

	Miles from Sun	Miles Diameter
Jupiter	over 483,000,000	about 90,000
Saturn	over 886,000,000	about 71,000
Uranus	1,783,000,000	30,000
Neptune	2,790,000,000	over 27,000
Pluto	3,670,000,000	over 3,000

Shuttle Wrap-Up: A Closed Case!

How do space shuttles withstand the extreme cold and heat of outer space? Do this heated experiment and find out. It's cool!

You need:

2 empty soda cans
clay (enough to close can openings)
2 small clear jars (remove labels)
2 thermometers
sheets of paper towels, paper bag, and aluminum foil (enough to wrap layers twice around one can)
scissors
2–4 rubber bands
paper and pencil
hot tap water
an assistant*

What to do:

Layer the three types of paper, with the foil in the middle, the paper bag on the inside and the paper toweling on the outside.

Fill both cans with hot tap water. Form two clay balls (about the size of a quarter) and press one against the hole in each can. Again, the clay ball should be pressed against the hole and not into it.

Work quickly as you wrap the paper layers around one of the cans (as you would wrap a blanket wrapper around a water heater) and secure it with rubber bands. The other can should remain as it is, without a wrapper.

*Four hands are faster than two and this experiment must be done quickly before the water cools and the thermometer temperatures change.

Patiently wait 30–40 minutes for the water to cool. Record the time.

Again, you must work quickly to get accurate results. First, make certain both thermometers register the same temperature. If not, run them under warm or cool water to get similar readings.

While leaving the wrapper on the can, quickly pour its contents, the water, into one of the jars. Do the same with the other can into the other jar. Place the cans behind each jar so as not to confuse the sample test waters. Place a thermometer in each jar

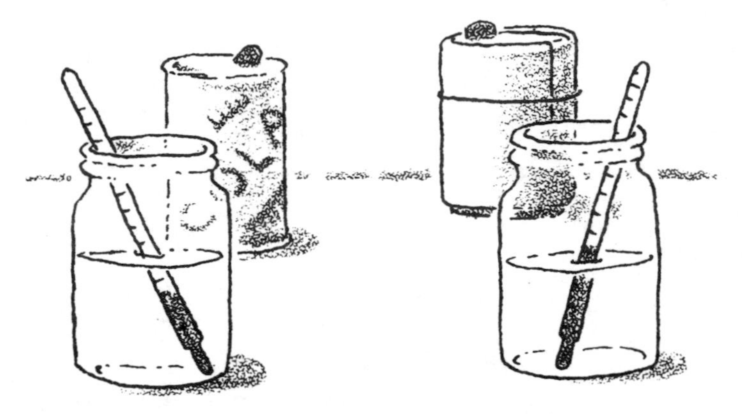

and let it stand for 2–3 minutes. Do not remove the thermometers from the jars when recording temperatures. Rather, press each to the side of the clear surface as you write down each number.

What happens:

The can with the wrapper showed a 3 to 5 degree recorded temperature difference. In other words, the water in the wrapped can was 3 to 5 degrees warmer than the can that was unwrapped.

Why:

There are extreme areas of heat and cold in outer

space, so spacecraft must be protected by wrapped blankets of insulating materials. These materials can be used to prevent or stop the loss of heat or even to cool.

Scientifically speaking, molecules vibrate more quickly in warm parts of a material and transfer heat energy to their slower-moving cousins in colder parts. This process is called conduction. Knowing about this process, space scientists use materials to absorb heat or to reflect it. In general, metals conduct or carry heat best, while wood, paper, plastic, water, and air are poor conductors.

THERMAL UNDERWEAR: A HEATED PROBLEM

In places where it's very cold, people often wear thermal underwear. These long coveralls, worn *under* regular clothes, are designed with air pockets to keep body heat in.

In "Shuttle Wrap-Up: A Closed Case!," we put a type of thermal wrap on a can, best described as thermal outerwear.

Try doing the same experiment, but substitute different layers and rearrange them in different ways. Does what is inside or outside the other layer make much difference in final results or do the results remain the same?

Also, create some new experiments with thermal outerwear. Try using different containers with different coverings and thicknesses to scientifically wrap up your final results.

Travel Agent

How well does heat travel through metal, plastic or wood? The right answer, important to space exploration, will keep you out of hot water.

You need:

metal object (fork, nail)
wooden object (pencil, stick)
plastic object (spoon, straw)
cup of very hot water
adult help with stove or microwave

What to do:

Have an adult heat a cup of water for this experiment (very hot water can cause a bad burn). Put all three objects in the cup of hot water, ends separated and upright, like wheel spokes.

Hot water!

After five minutes, carefully touch the middle of the objects, where they meet the lip of the cup. Also, remove each object and feel the ends that were covered with the hot water. Of the three, which feels the warmest?

What happens:

Parts of the metal object feel warmer than those of the wooden or plastic object.

Why:

Metals are better conductors of heat than plastic or wood. Electrons are looser in metals and can carry heat better. This explains why the metal object in our experiment felt warmer than the plastic or wood.

Now, you can see how this information would be helpful and very important to space scientists for insulating or protecting spacecraft and astronauts for the extreme temperatures of outer space.

Space Food: Can't Keep It Down!

Want to pretend you're an astronaut, and eat space-style? Enjoy this easy and fun experiment.

You need:

- 1 package instant breakfast drink powder
- 1 quart-size freezer bag (the kind that locks closed)
- milk
- bendable straw

What to do:

Pour the drink mix into the freezer bag. Add milk, no more than one-third full. Close the bag securely and shake thoroughly. Open one small corner of the bag and insert the straw. Sip your astromeal!

What happens:

The food-in-a-bag demonstrates how food is eaten in space—sucked through a straw.

Why:

Astronauts need to keep their foods *contained* in outer space. Without closed pouches, liquids and other loose foods would simply separate, and float away—all around the cabin! Messy, huh?

Space foods are dehydrated (dried), like our powdered breakfast drink, and rehydrated (water added) in outer space.

What next:

Look for other dried foods found here on Earth and rehydrate them by adding water or milk.

Also, experiment with ice cream and other juices and foods that you can serve and eat space-style, using plastic bag containers. It's a neat and fun way to eat—without all the mess.

Man Your Station!

Make a simple space station and then man it, or place a crew member or members on its deck, whirl it, and, learn what centrifugal force can really do.

You need:

4 toilet paper tubes
one toothpaste box or similar carton
2–3 marbles, erasers, or other small objects
string, 36 inches (90cm)
scissors
tape

What to do:

Cut a rectangular opening in the narrow side of the box, leaving an inch of cardboard at either end.

Have someone poke a hole on each side of the box, thread the string through both ends, and tie each side off. You now should have a string handle and a rectangular opening in the box.

With tape, attach a pair of cardboard tubes to each side. You should have what looks like an opened box with a pair of doubled-tube wings.

Last, place one object, followed by two to four, inside the box, or module, of your space station. While holding the string, rock the model slowly, then make several full-circle swings. Start the string whirling slowly, gradually increase the speed, and then, very slowly, come to a stop.

What happens:

With a slow, rocking swing, the objects move and rattle around in the box. With a faster, full, over-the-head whirl, the objects stay in place and do not move, while a slower, coming-to-a-stop-type swing starts the objects moving and eventually they fly from the box.

Why:

The overall force that kept the objects in your make-believe space station module from flying out was called centrifugal.

When you rapidly whirled the station above your head, you pulled the objects inside the box towards you (centripetal force; see "Spooling Around") and the objects, in turn, pulled outward or away from you.

DESIGNER CRAFT

To design a more authentic, realistic space station, bring out marker pens, scissors, cardboard, toilet/paper towel tubes, tape, string—and lots of imagination. The illustration on this page will help you.

For starters, use a paper towel tube for the different parts or modules of your craft. Also, since the tube is similar to the cylinder shape of a real station, this will add realism.

Then, have someone cut out two or three rectangular pieces from the ends or middle of the tube. This will make the modules look authentic or real. Too, you may wish it to hold objects and put it into orbit as you did in "Man Your Station!"

Draw circular and side lines to show the different modular parts. Add rectangular cardboard pieces to your model to show the many solar panels that are attached to such crafts.

Last, if you wish, attach string and astronauts, and put your craft into orbit as you did in "Man Your Station!" Have fun!

SO YOU WANT TO BE AN ASTRONAUT

The future is waiting for you. If your goal is to be a part of it, *out there*, now is a good time to start thinking of how to turn your dream of going into space into reality.

Here, from the agencies involved in space work and exploration, is information on how you can take your place as an astronaut.

ASTRONAUT SELECTION AND TRAINING

In the future, the United States, with its international partners Japan, Canada, and the European Space Agency, will operate a manned Space Station. From that orbiting depot, explorers will continue on their journeys to the moon and Mars. As these plans come closer to reality, the need for qualified spaceflight professionals will increase.

To fill the upcoming need, NASA accepts applications for the Astronaut Candidate Program on a continuous basis. Candidates are selected as needed, normally every two years, for pilot and mission-specialist categories. Both civilian and military personnel are considered for the program. Civilians may apply at any time. Military personnel must apply through their parent service and be nominated by their branch of service to transfer to NASA.

The astronaut candidate selection process was developed to select highly qualified individuals for human space programs. For mission specialists and pilot-astronaut candidates, there are several educational and experience requirements: at least a bachelor's degree from an accredited institution in engineering, biological science, physical science, or mathematics. Three years of related, progressively responsible professional experience must follow the degree. An advanced degree is desirable and may be substituted for all or part of the experience requirement (i.e., master's degree = 1 year of work experience, doctoral degree = 3 years of experience).

Applicants who meet the basic qualifications are evaluated by discipline panels during a week-long process of personal interviews, thorough medical evaluations, and orientation.

Selected applicants are designated "astronaut candidates" and are assigned to the astronaut office at Johnson Space Center for a one-year training-and-evaluation period. During this time, candidates take part in the astronaut training program designed to develop the knowledge and skills required for formal mission training upon selection for a flight, and are assigned technical or scientific responsibilities. However, selection as a candidate does not ensure selection as an astronaut.

Final selection is based on satisfactory completion of the one-year program. Civilian candidates who successfully complete the training and evaluation, and are selected as astronauts, are expected to remain with NASA for at least five years.

Portions reprinted courtesy of the National Aeronautics and Space Administration and the Lyndon B. Johnson Space Center, Houston, Texas.

ROCKETRY: THE THREE R'S (READY! REACTION! REPLAY!)

The many mini-experiments in this chapter are based on a balloon-straw-string rocket. You may have seen balloon-string rockets in experiment books before, but not the way we've presented them.

We've absolutely shot the works! We've used balloons, weights, balances, and counterbalances to explain the concepts or ideas of thrust, acceleration, deceleration, and booster and retro rockets.

You'll be doing experiments with rockets, space shuttles, and retrorockets in mind. We've even added a jet-propelled toy car for fast thinkers, and you won't need expensive or dangerous propellants, or fuels—it's all 100% balloon power.

So, power up! You'll need lots of balloons, both large round and oblong ones, and perhaps a helper, but you'll soon be bursting with fun and ideas. And all the experiments are fuel-proof!

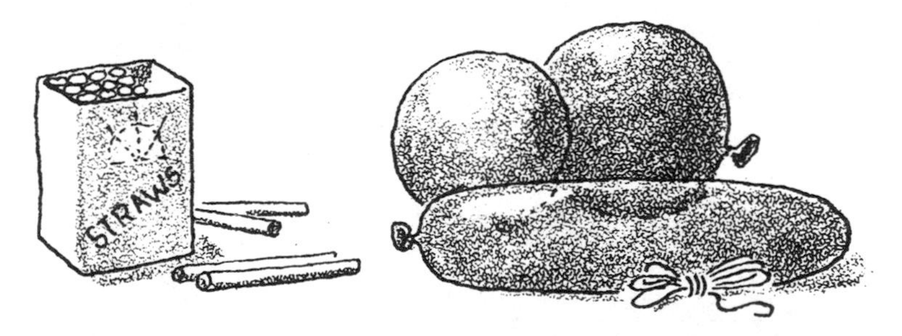

Rocket Scientists Don't Fuel Around

Space scientists are very serious when it comes to getting a spacecraft off the ground. Fuel is a very important part of any space launch and our "fuel"-proof experiment will have you sputtering, hissing, and roaring with excitement. An assistant is recommended.

You need:

aluminum foil (enough for a tightly packed 5-inch (13cm) rocket)
a 1-pt. (500ml) plastic beverage bottle filled with vinegar (5% or more acidity)
coffee filter
3 tsp. baking soda
3 rubber bands

NOTE: This experiment can be messy; *do it outdoors*!

What to do:

Place three teaspoons of baking soda on the coffee filter and spread out evenly into a long column. Fold over evenly to form a long tube package, and secure with rubber bands. This will represent your fuel package. Pack the aluminum foil to form a 5-inch (13cm) rocket, making certain the bottom end fits snugly but not to tightly into the bottle. It should still be loose enough to move up and down. Take your bottle of vinegar, fuel package, and rocket outside to a location that can be easily washed down.

The next steps must be done carefully and quickly. Make certain the long fuel tube is not broken or leaking and can be easily inserted into the bottle.

Next, drop the fuel package into the bottle, quickly followed by the rocket. When the chemical reaction occurs, poke the rocket down into the bottle and watch what happens.

Continue to poke the rocket down into the bottle until the reaction stops.

What happens:

The vinegar and baking soda chemically combine to produce CO_2 gas. The gas, in turn, overflows from the bottle, hisses, steams, and slightly moves the rocket.

Why:

Your model rocket on its launch pad (bottle) simulates or copies a real rocket or spacecraft launched into outer space.

In a real craft, two liquid fuels are combined and explode, causing pressure and giving the craft its lift or thrust.

The chemical reaction—hissing, steam, and overflow and slight lift when the model rocket is pushed back into the bottle—copies the built-up pressure, exhaust, and lift of the real thing.

DESIGNING A ROCKET

How about being creative and designing special features on your 5-inch (13cm) aluminum rocket? And, since the rocket is waterproof, you can use it over and over. Better yet, why not try modeling extra rockets of different designs and sizes for future launches.

With a little imagination, waterproof permanent markers, extra aluminum foil, straws and other waterproof household materials, you can do much to change the design and shape of your rockets.

Try forming strips of foil in separate bands around the width of your missile to show the different parts or stages of the rocket. Also, reshape the nose of your model or construct tail fins. You might even add booster or end rockets (straws work best) to make your craft look more realistic.

Last, use permanent marker pens to draw U.S.A. or other logos or signs on your project.

Have fun!

MAINTENANCE CREW

It's nice to have assistants, a "maintenance crew," to help set up the following experiments. There's lots to do: tightening rocket lines, cutting tape off straws, inflating and adjusting balloons, etc. But with help, you'll be able to shoot the works quite easily.

Shuttled About

Watch the space capsule fall off your model rocket as it reaches its target. Although modern spacecraft use a space shuttle system with a plane-like orbiter, your simple rocket will demonstrate how one part of a spacecraft can be launched into outer space with the help of another.

You need:

outdoor location
an assistant
a drinking straw
large long balloon
large Styrofoam cup
paper and pencil
thread
tape
paper clip
scissors
watch with second hand
clip, clothespin, or push pin (see "Line Item")

What to do:

Tie 4 to 5 yards (or meters) of thread lengthwise from one chair or object to another as a *free*, or removable, line. On one end of the line, thread the straw (see "Line Item" on page 118). An assistant is recommended for the following steps.

Blow up the balloon, twist the end, and clip it. With a very long piece of tape, fasten the balloon to the underside of the straw, making certain the hole faces the chair. Next, loosely fit the cup over the nose, or front, of the balloon. This will represent earlier space capsules, which were fitted onto the end of rockets.

You now are ready to launch your rocket. Remove the paper clip from the balloon while holding the end of it closed. When ready, release the balloon and time how long it takes your rocket to leave its launch pad and reach its target.

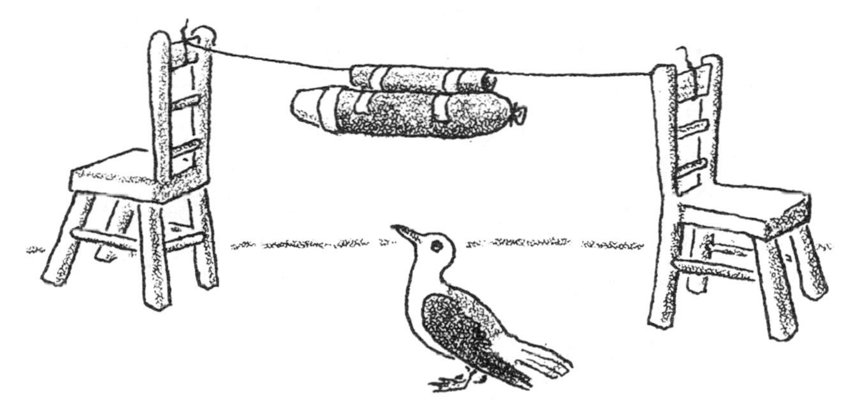

What happens:
When released, the balloon races along the string and reaches its target while the cup or capsule falls off.

Why:
Your balloon rocket demonstrates the law of Sir Isaac Newton: for every action there is an equal and opposite reaction. Your rocket shows how the principles of jet propulsion work. The backward push of the air escaping from the balloon propels or pushes the balloon forward.

LINE ITEM

The clip, clothespin, or push pin is used to attach or pin one end of the rocket-balloon thread line from one object to another, e.g., chair. One end of the line can be permanently tied to an object but the other should be free. This is done so that balloon rockets (slipped on a thread line through a straw attached to a balloon) can be changed when needed. Since there are many mini experiments with our balloon rockets, this free line should be helpful.

To easily get the thread through the straw, tie one end of it around the head of a straight pin and drop it through the straw. Leave the pin on the thread to act as a plumb or weighted line. The pin can be draped over a push pin or attached by a clip to another object.

Booster Shot

Now that you've got the hang of it, why not try a booster shot? You'll keep the same setup and do the same experiment as you just did in "Shuttled About," but now you'll add an extra balloon, or booster rocket. Will it make any difference in the rate of speed and time your rocket reaches its target? Be a big shot and find out!

You need:
materials from "Shuttled About," plus
a second long balloon
an assistant

What to do:
Again, blow up the original balloon taped to the underside of the straw. (If the balloon is now too stretched out or doesn't work well, replace it with a new one.) Twist the end and clip it.

Now, add a new long balloon to the side of the original balloon. Again, tape, twist, and clip the end of the balloon.

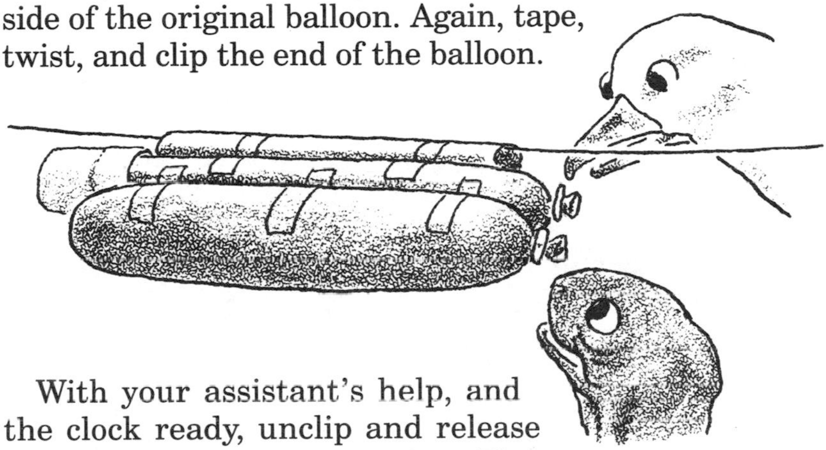

With your assistant's help, and the clock ready, unclip and release *both* balloons at the *same time*. Time how long it takes for your booster rocket to reach its target. Is there a big difference between the booster's time and the one in "Shuttled About"?

What happens:
Your balloon rocket, with its booster rocket, races along the string with more force than your original rocket.

Why:
With two rockets, the jet propulsion rate is doubled and thus the rate of travel is faster.

Completely Exhausted

You'll love this effect we've created for your balloon rocket. We've simulated, or copied, the real thrust and propulsion of the jet rocket engine. We've also given you an idea how the stages of a rocket work. Now, as a surprise bonus, we're adding a bit of fake smoke for realism! The materials are easy to find and we absolutely guarantee it won't leave you *exhaust*ed.

You need:
1 teaspoon flour
small funnel
spoon

What to do:
Do this experiment as you did the others. However, before you blow up the balloon and attach it to the straw, place the funnel inside the opening of the uninflated balloon and fill it with about a spoonful of flour. Use the spoon to stir the flour around in the funnel and into the balloon.

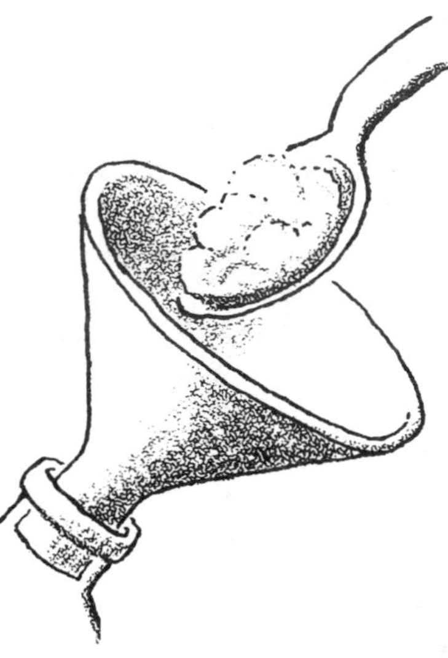

Inflate the balloon, shake it so the flour reaches the opening, attach it to the straw, tie it off with the clip, and get ready to shoot the works.

What happens:
If done correctly, the balloon rocket races along the string, leaving a trail of smoke behind it!

Four Going Retro

Now, using the same thread line and materials used in "Shuttled About," try doing these next four mini experiments on retrorockets, those small secondary or additional rockets that produce a thrust *opposite* to that of the main rocket. Retrorockets are often used to slow down a spacecraft's reentry or to *soft land*. You can also try extending your thread line, buy larger balloons, or increase the number of balloons for added thrust.

Get your whole family, or at least a friend, involved in these experiments. You'll need the help of an assistant anyway! Now get moving...and have a blast!

Retrorocket I: Watch the Tube!

With cardboard tubes alongside, this rocket looks and acts like a real one—with retrorockets!

You need:

line hookup with one straw
1 oblong balloon
1 paper clip
2 toilet paper tubes
tape
scissors

What to do:

With tape, attach the two tubes high along the sides of an inflated balloon. (HINT: It's much easier to attach the tape to the inside of the tubes first, then lay the other ends of the tape against the balloon.) Attach the balloon to the straw, release the balloon from an end of the line, and observe what happens.

What happens:

The balloon pushes or shoots down the line, but with less force, and does not reach the end of it.

Why:
The tubes, like retrorockets, act as a counter-force, a force or action acting *against* the main thrust of the rocket balloon. This, in turn, slows down the main thrust of the rocket balloon and makes it unable to reach its target.

Retrorocket II: A Perfect Roll Model

Now try the same experiment, but with a difference!

You need:
line hookup with one straw
1 oblong balloon
1 toilet paper tube
3–4 sheets newspaper (the inner, circular-size are best)
tape
scissors

What to do:
Inflate the balloon and, with tape, securely fasten the tube to the bottom of it and then to the straw.

Next, roll and tape the newspapers into a tight cylinder and place them into the attached balloon tube. Release the balloon from one end of the line and observe what happens.

What happens:
The rocket moves only to the middle of the thread line, and then stops.

Why:
The retrorocket-like tube-cylinder, due to its weight, acted as a greater counter or opposite force, and it slowed down more than its tubed cousin.

Retrorocket III: Bully for You!

The balloon rocket in this experiment is a regular bully, but it shows you, forcefully, the opposite thrust of a retrorocket.

You need:

line hookup with 2 straws
3 oblong balloons
3 paper clips
scissors
tape

What to do:

Thread two straws at the beginning of the removable end of the free thread line.

Next, inflate three oblong balloons—two fully inflated, the other, half inflated. With tape, attach the two fully inflated balloons together on one of the straws; then twist and clip the end of each balloon. Do the same with the half-inflated balloon on the other straw. It's important that the balloons are *facing* each other, with back openings facing the ends of each line.

Hold your balloons about a quarter of the distance away from the end line while your assistant does the same with the half-inflated balloon.

At an announced signal, release the balloons... and watch the action carefully

What happens:
The two-balloon rocket pushes the half-inflated balloon to the other side of the line.

Why:
The two-balloon rocket represents a forceful retroocket that slows and forcefully pushes the smaller, main rocket back to its end line.

Retrorocket IV: You're Canceled!

What will happen if two fully inflated balloons, moving in the same direction, meet?

You need:
line hookup with 2 straws
2 paper clips
2 oblong balloons
tape

What to do:
Repeat the steps in "Retrorocket III: Bully for You!" but replace these balloons with two fully inflated balloons facing each other with openings behind and facing the end lines.

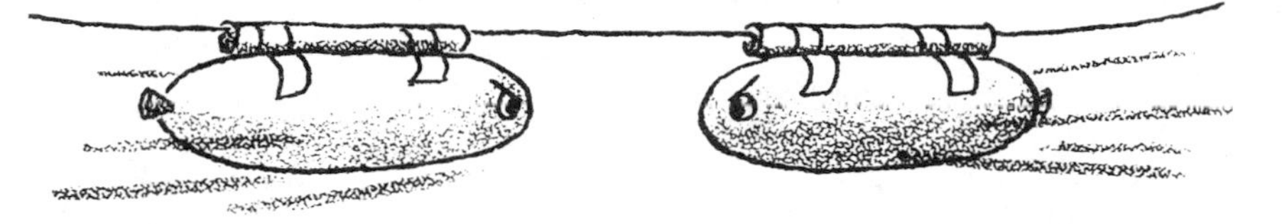

What happens:
The two balloons shoot to the middle of the line and stop.

Why:
The thrust or push from each balloon was the same and, when they met, pushed against each other, stopping or canceling one another out.

FOREGOING RETRO

A toy car moving in one direction can be redirected into an opposite direction. How? It's not rocketry, but a *reverse* trick using counter-forces.

You need:

a toy mini car
a 6-inch (15cm) wide strip of cardboard
the floor near a wall
long cardboard tube
paper clip
round balloon
tape

What to do:

Fold the strip of cardboard in half or in thirds lengthwise to make a walled track. Push it up against a wall. Then blow up the balloon and knot or twist it closed. Clip or tape the balloon to the lower wall and floor, or to the track, so it becomes a barrier at the end of it.

Hold the long tube at a downward angle, adjusting it as needed at the track opening opposite the balloon, and drop the car into it.

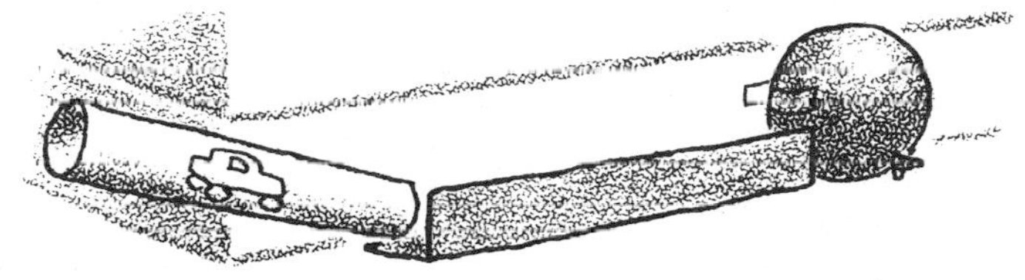

What happens:

The car slides down the tube and onto the track. When it hits the balloon, the car is pushed backwards on the track. It's *not* a retrorocket, but another way a forward-moving object can be sent in another or opposite direction.

Index